7 ACTIONS OF A
WISE WOMAN

A Complete Woman Series

SORINES LOPEZ

PRESS

ISBN 9781498473620

www.xulonpress.com

CHAPTERS

Introduction xi

Action 1 | Reflect 19
Action 2 | Courage to Act 31
Action 3 | Sacrifice 45
Action 4 | Humble yourself and speak with wisdom 55
Action 5 | Forgiveness 75
Action 6 | Stand in the Gap 89
Action 7 | Rejoice 101

What Will Your Story Be? 113
Acknowledgments 119
About the Author................................. 129

DEDICATION

I dedicate this book to my amazing mother, Digna Gonzalez. She is not a woman of many words, but every word she says is certainly worth listening to.

Mom, I remember the day you and I were driving in my car and we were having a conversation about parenting. As we were talking, your eyes filled with tears as you said, "I don't think I did enough as a mom." I told you that day and I will say it again publicly – "Mom, you went above and beyond for all of us. There was nothing more you could have done for us growing up. Our mistakes are not your fault. You have taught us, disciplined when necessary, and loved us unconditionally."

Mom, you have always created a safe, loving and fun home for the eight of us. We are who we are today because of your love, patience, spiritual guidance and wisdom.

Mom, you continue to love us, and that makes us rich. You share Jesus with us, through your words and actions, and that makes us eternally blessed!

Thank you for loving and believing in me the way you do. I've heard it said a mother's love is the closest to God's love. Well, they were thinking of you when that was said.

Mom, I love you more than words can ever express. #BESTMOMEVER

Joyful is the person who finds wisdom, the one
who gains understanding.
For wisdom is more profitable than silver, and her wages
are better than gold. Wisdom is more precious than rubies;
nothing you desire can compare with her. She offers you
long life in her right hand, and riches and honor in her left.
She will guide you down delightful paths; all her ways are
satisfying. Wisdom is a tree of life to those who embrace
her; happy are those who hold her tightly.
Proverbs 3:13-18

What are the actions that make a woman wise?

Often it is not one single moment, but rather a series of events that led up to that moment and what she then decides to do with that moment.

The standard can be found in scripture: *"A wise woman builds her home, but a foolish woman tears it down with her own hands." Proverbs 14:1*

That verse doesn't need much explanation. However, allow me to share some actions that I have found to be very useful in my life. Actions like reflecting, acting, making sacrifices, forgiving, being humble, speaking with wisdom, standing in the gap and rejoicing. I believe that in sharing these actions with you, they will help you be the wise woman Proverbs talks about. To help illustrate, we can learn a lot from two amazing and different women of the Bible: Abigail and Esther. Although their stories are very different, you will notice the same actions used to help make wise decisions.

In case you are unfamiliar with Esther, let me bring you up to speed. Have you heard the rags-to-riches story of Annie and Daddy Warbucks? Well, with a few tweaks you could easily cast Esther as the Jewish Annie belting out the lyrics to 'Tomorrow.' She was an orphan girl being raised by her cousin's family. There was nothing special happening in her ordinary life. That is, until the queen decided to embarrass the king and suddenly a decree went out requesting that young women in her town present themselves for a sort of tryout. One of them would be selected the new queen. Whether she wanted to be queen or not, Esther becomes queen and at the instruction of Mordecai, she leaves out the detail that she is Jewish.

Abigail is an example of a women whose actions were less publicized and popularized — they might seem quite insignificant at the time, however, these actions prove to shape wise women just the same. While Abigail was living her life, she had no idea there were events, years in the making, that were taking place and that would soon present her with a choice. As the saying goes, she would need to carefully consider the options and choose wisely.

One such year-in-the-making event that soon would cross paths with hers was the life of a man named David. You may have heard the name King David, or the stories of the mighty warrior, David. Well, before either of those came about, there was a young shepherd boy tending to his sheep. David experienced his own series of events and faced choices that made him into the David who lives on today in stories and sermons.

As a shepherd boy, David cared for his sheep with passion and boldness. As he protected the sheep against predators like lions and bears, he developed courage and confidence in the Lord's favor and protection. This same courage and confidence emerged when he encountered Goliath, the Philistine giant that had the Israelite soldiers cowering with fear.

1 Samuel 10:17-27, the Prophet Samuel anoints Saul King over Israel. Fast forward to chapter 13 Verses 13-14 Saul disobeyed God's command and Samuel said to Saul, *"How foolish!" You have not kept the command the LORD your God gave you. Had you kept it, the LORD would have established your kingdom over Israel forever. But now your kingdom must end, for the LORD has sought out a man after his own heart. The LORD has already appointed him to be the leader of his people, because you have not kept the LORD's command.*

In the 16th chapter we are told that one day, the Prophet Samuel enters David's father, Jesse's, house in search of the next King of Israel. There, he interviews all of David's brothers before concluding they are not 'The One.' Jesse reluctantly informs Samuel he does have one more son, who couldn't possibly be the Lord's choice for king. Nonetheless, Samuel asks him to fetch the missing son. David presents himself to Samuel and the Prophet anoints him to be the next king of Israel. As King Saul later became jealous of David's newfound fame as a giant slayer and mighty warrior, David's humility, when given the opportunity to take Saul's life, prompts him to spare it instead.

So how do the lives of a shepherd boy-made-warrior and the wife of a wealthy man cross paths? The answer is in 1 Samuel 25.

> [1] *Now Samuel died, and all Israel gathered for his funeral. They buried him at his house in Ramah. Then David moved down to the wilderness of Maon.* [2] *There was a wealthy man from Maon who owned property near the town of Carmel. He had 3,000 sheep and 1,000 goats, and it was sheep-shearing time.* [3] *This man's name was Nabal, and his wife, Abigail, was a sensible and beautiful woman. But Nabal, a descendant of Caleb, was crude and mean in all his dealings.*
>
> [4] *When David heard that Nabal was shearing his sheep,* [5] *he sent ten of his young men to Carmel with this message for Nabal:* [6] *"Peace and prosperity to you, your family, and everything you own!* [7] *I am told that it is sheep-shearing time. While your shepherds stayed among us near Carmel, we never harmed them, and nothing was ever stolen from them.* [8] *Ask your own men, and they will tell you this is true. So would you be kind to us, since we have come at a time of celebration? Please share any*

provisions you might have on hand with us and with your friend David." [9]*David's young men gave this message to Nabal in David's name, and they waited for a reply.*

[10]*"Who is this fellow David?" Nabal sneered to the young men. "Who does this son of Jesse think he is? There are lots of servants these days who run away from their masters.* [11]*Should I take my bread and my water and my meat that I've slaughtered for my shearers and give it to a band of outlaws who come from who knows where?"*

[12]*So David's young men returned and told him what Nabal had said.* [13]*"Get your swords!" was David's reply as he strapped on his own. Then 400 men started off with David, and 200 remained behind to guard their equipment.*

And so the story has built up to this moment. David and his four hundred mighty men were on their way to eliminate Nabal and his household — I'm talking remove from the face of the Earth. Why? David was hungry and Nabal didn't give him food. He felt disrespected by Nabal's response and became enraged.

Unfortunately for Nabal, he didn't have the wise teaching of my mother Digna to guide him. My mother told me before I was married to never start important or sensitive conversations with my husband when he walked through the door after a long day of work. She would tell me, "Let him come in, take his shoes off, relax, feed him and then ease your way into a conversation."

She was a stay-at-home mom and there were eight of us children, so this practice proved valuable early on in her marriage. With eight children, all within 10 years of each other (my dad likes to say there wasn't television at that time), it wasn't like he was coming home to a quiet house. My mom would be sure he had time to settle before he got the day's play-by-play. I'm sure there were times when she wanted to say, "I'm glad you're here because I need a break. These kids are driving me crazy." However, I don't recall her ever doing that. You don't celebrate more than 50 years of marriage without wisdom. But unfortunately, Nabal had no such advice. He did not take anything into consideration before he replied to David's men.

Abigail was home minding her business. David was living in the wilderness fleeing from King Saul. Neither of them knew their paths would soon cross.

Fear of the Lord is the foundation of true knowledge,
but fools despise wisdom and discipline.
Proverbs 1:7

ACTION 1 | REFLECT

Meanwhile, one of Nabal's servants went to Abigail and told her, "David sent messengers from the wilderness to greet our master, but he screamed insults at them. These men have been very good to us, and we never suffered any harm from them. Nothing was stolen from us the whole time they were with us. In fact, day and night they were like a wall of protection to us and the sheep. You need to know this and figure out what to do, for there is going to be trouble for our master and his whole family. He's so ill-tempered that no one can even talk to him!" (1 Samuel 25:14-17)

How many times have you reacted instead of reflected? You heard some news, didn't let the news settle, didn't think to get the other side of the story because what difference would that make, right? If you're honest, you're probably nodding your head up and down. Looking back at those moments, how many times did you regret what you said or what you did? Careful, don't hurt your neck. You're not alone. I've been guilty of this many times and I still catch myself, sometimes a little too late.

The truth is, many of us don't reflect as much as we should. Instead, we react and hurt others and ourselves. There is a difference between the two. Webster's Dictionary defines them like this:

Reflect: To think quietly and calmly

React: To change in response to a stimulus

The truth is, many of us don't reflect as much as we should. Instead, we react and hurt others and ourselves.

When you react without listening, thinking, or asking questions, you are left with actions and words that could have been avoided if you simply would have counted to 10, so to speak, then taken time to listen.

In order for Abigail to know what was going on, she had to listen. She had to pay close attention as her servant came to her, probably out of breath from running to warn her. I can picture Abigail saying, "Slow down, catch your breath. Wait, did I hear you say David and his men were coming to kill us? Why? What is going on?" Abigail's life was turning upside down and inside out, and all she had were questions running through her mind. She was trying to process the information as quickly as possible. She had to stop and reflect because how she proceeded could save or kill her family.

If it hasn't happened already, get ready because the day will come when you will be presented with news and the ability to turn off the spotlight that is shining upon you will be completely out of your control. Eyes will be locked on you to see how you handle the situation. In those moments, I pray you take the time to reflect before you react.

That news could be day-to-day news, for example, like the check engine light comes on, the principal from your child's school calls, or you've been offered a promotion at work. Whatever the details might be, good or bad, if we are wise (or want to be wise), we should take the time to reflect before we react. Reflection is very important because it allows us to see the bigger picture.

Then there are moments when you are hit with life-changing news. You go from enjoying a beautiful, sunny day where you're breathing in the fresh air to your stomach turning and your heart aching because of what you just heard.

I am thankful to God I am a woman. Most of the time I am thankful for my emotions, too. There have been times when I have been able to control my emotions and there have been times when I have let them get the best of me. I've heard my husband preach and say, "If you don't control your emotions,

Don't allow your emotion's to cause you to act unwisely.

they will control you." I don't claim him to be the author of it but there is a lot of truth in that statement. Don't allow your emotion's to cause you to act unwisely.

I've heard statements like this before from women: "Well, I'm a woman so I can't help it." You can help it! It's up to you to either be as level-headed as possible or act like a child in the candy store having a tantrum because you're not getting what you want.

How about this one, "You know how women are?" One of my close friends shared with me that after being a stay-at-home mom for many years, she took a full-time job. She said she was probably home for 20 minutes and she had already yelled at her son at least four times. Her husband noticed this behavior and lovingly brought it to her attention, to which she responded, "I am who I am." She looked right at me and said, "Why did I say that? I don't talk like that." So my question is why resort to an abrupt response rather than reflect before we reply?

The one thing all women have in common is we are all different and unique, but we all have to strive to be the wise woman God has called us to be. Remember Proverbs 14:1?

We need to be women who build our home with words of encouragement and affirmation. It's not that we won't yell at our children. Lord, help us be better with that. Let's learn to reflect before we speak to our children so that we can uplift and encourage them, especially when they make a mistake. Remember, we were not and are not perfect.

Let's look at Esther. She was informed that her cousin Mordecai was in great mourning and she wanted to know why.

> *Then Esther sent for Hathach, one of the king's eunuchs who had been appointed as her attendant. She ordered him to go to Mordecai and find out what was troubling him and why he was in mourning. So Hathach went out to Mordecai in the square in front of the palace gate. Mordecai told him the whole story, including the exact amount of money Haman had promised to pay into the royal treasury for the destruction of the Jews. Mordecai gave Hathach a copy of the decree issued in Susa that called for the death of all Jews. He asked Hathach to show it to Esther and explain the situation to her. He also asked Hathach to direct her to go to the king to beg for mercy and plead for her people. So Hathach returned to Esther with Mordecai's message. (Esther 4:5-9)*

When the news reaches Esther, she responds, and I'm paraphrasing: "If anyone approaches the king without being summoned, he or she will be put to death unless the king extends the gold scepter and spares their life. It's been thirty days and he hasn't called for me.... what makes you think

I can make a difference?" Esther knew enough to reflect, because reacting immediately may have gotten her killed.

Esther is living out the life of luxury in the palace. She is presented with the news that her husband, King Xerxes, who has no idea she's Jewish, has just put his seal of approval on Haman's decree calling for the slaughter of Jews. Not only that, but Mordecai, who had pretty much been like a father figure in her life, is now asking her to plead with the king on behalf of the Jews. That sounds like a whole lot of news to reflect on, but if you remember Esther quickly sums it up: "What makes you think I can make a difference here?"

I believe we need a Mordecai in our lives. Someone who will encourage us and help position us for greatness. Someone who will, when the time comes, shake us up and cause us to reflect on why we are where we are. There should be someone to remind us that it's not about us, it's about HIM! That is exactly what Mordecai does in his response to Esther again, I'm paraphrasing: "Don't think because you're in the palace you're going to be spared. If you choose to be silent, one way or another, relief and deliverance will come from another place for all of us, but you will die. And who knows, maybe you have come to this royal position for such a time as this?"

Mordecai's words laid out the details for Esther just as the servant's words laid out the details for Abigail. Whether they wanted to admit it or not, they were both facing death.

But neither of them did anything to bring this ill fate upon themselves. Life is not fair! It was time to reflect.

Mordecai helped her reflect when he said, *"Who knows if perhaps you were made queen for just such a time as this?"* (Esther 4:14) She realized that if she was going to present herself before King Xerxes, she couldn't do it alone. She had to have someone greater on her side; she had to bring this to God.

> *"Go and gather together all the Jews of Susa and*
> *fast for me. Do not eat or drink for three days,*
> *night or day. My maids and I will do the same.*
> *And then, though it is against the law, I will go*
> *in to see the king. If I must die, I must die."*
> *(Esther 4:16)*

Esther's reflection here is a key point of every wise woman. As women, many times we try to do things on our own because we think nobody cares the way we care, or if we don't do it, then who will? The

Reflecting should cause us to fall to our knees.

downside to this is burnout, frustration, playing the blame game and many heartaches, as well as headaches. Yes, we can argue and say God knows what we're going through, but that does not give us a reason to not seek His counsel. Reflecting should cause us to fall to our knees. If that is the only thing you get out of this book, I'm ok with that.

Girlfriend, we have no problem spending hours talking to our friends over the phone or texting about what is going on. Sadly, there are even those who will choose to hang their dirty laundry on Facebook. Yes, I had to go there, and let me state very clearly, that is never a wise choice. The one we should take our situation to is God, though He is often the last one we turn to. We need to change this in our lives.

What if Abigail had decided to tell all her friends about her husband's surly mouth? If it is easy for you to complain to your friends about your husband's shortcomings, I'd like to offer some advice that I received from my mother. It was early in my marriage and I went to my mom to complain about my husband, Peter. As I'm running my mouth, my mom with her sweet, calming spirit stops me and says, "You need to be very careful how you speak about your husband to others. I know you're speaking freely to me because I'm your mother, but you need to catch yourself when you're with your girlfriends." Again she was right! My goal in complaining was to shift all the blame on him. I wanted her to just tell me I was right and he was wrong. Her words helped me to reflect on myself. I needed to look at the plank in my eye and not the speck in his. Wise women uplift and encourage their husbands in and out of their presence. This can only come through reflecting upon what is pouring out of our mouths.

Esther could have thrown a giant banner out the palace window and said, "I'm Jewish, tell the king how much you like me if you want me to live." Not everything you hear is meant to be broadcasted to the masses. How different would these stories have been if these women had gone down the common road? What we do with the news we receive is important! What is equally important is how long we take to reflect.

As we continue reading their stories, we find Esther takes longer to reflect than Abigail. Why? Well that's an easy one to answer. Different details take different lengths of time during the reflection period. If Esther reflected without taking the necessary time to seek God for those three days, her story wouldn't have turned out the way God planned it. If Abigail had said, "Well he's the man and that's that," her story also would have turned out differently.

Don't misunderstand me, if your house is on fire, don't reflect and wait to see what you should do. Hurry up. Get out of there and call 911! If you get news that a loved one was in an accident and is being rushed to the hospital, get to the hospital. Use the time it takes you to get there wisely, to reflect and pray. Don't worry. (Yes, easier said than done, I know). As hard as it may seem, try to focus on God and His promises for you and those around you, just as Abigail and Esther did. Worrying and panicking won't make the situation better, but rather can make it worse.

In 2004, I was presented with some ideas that could have steered me down a different path. Reflecting was vital. When the Lord spoke to me and said, "There are women who are hungry and you need to feed them. There are women who are thirsty and you need to give them drink," I had no idea how I was to get this done. I just felt like I had to. Thankfully, I acted with wisdom and reflected. I would go before the Lord and say, "I heard what you said, but how do I do it?"

I really didn't understand what I was being asked to do. I'm sure David, the shepherd boy, had a similar dilemma when he was told he was going to be king. He probably said to himself, "Thanks for the promise, thanks for the plan, but God how about a road map on how to get there?"

I had no doubt I had heard from God, but He wasn't showing me the full picture. I knew God was asking me to do something with and for women, but what and how? I had no idea God was planting an idea that would become a vision and shortly after a reality known as Complete Woman Conferences. I had to learn to be patient in the process. So I did the things I knew to do – pray, meditate, speak with my husband and when the time was right, speak with key people God put in my path. I'm telling you, prayer is SO important. It got me through reflecting and prepared me for action.

If you haven't noticed, the enemy is around the corner and all he wants to do is destroy you and your generation. He wants to steal your joy and your peace. Wake up! Reflect!

Make war against him through prayer. Seek God and get His direction. Your husband and children are worth the fight.

Abigail had David and his mighty men marching toward her house. Esther had a decree, which meant death to the entire Jewish race. It was time to reflect, it was time to seek some guidance from God.

There is a time to reflect and there is a time to act. I like how Solomon says it in Ecclesiastes 3:1, "For everything there is a season, a time for every activity under heaven." I also like how Isaiah words it, "Those who trust in the Lord will find new strength." (Isaiah 40:31) Another translation says, "Those who wait on the Lord shall renew their strength." There is wisdom in reflecting!

For the Lord grants wisdom! From his mouth
come knowledge and understanding.
Proverbs 2:6

ACTION 2 |
COURAGE TO ACT

*You need to know this and figure out what to do,
for there is going to be trouble for our master
and his whole family. He's so ill-tempered that
no one can even talk to him!" (1 Samuel 25:17)*

Once you have taken the necessary time to reflect, then what? Great question. The answer is, you act. While reflecting and acting are two different things, we must also remember that for a wise woman, these go hand in hand. In Abigail's case, understanding how to react was a bit easier. David was hungry. Ok then, let's feed him. Esther didn't have it that easy.

Our time of reflection could be compared to an army drawing up battle plans, or a sports team going over a game plan. It's preparation for what is to come. You must develop a plan (reflect), but after that you must take action or nothing will change. Reflection should cause us to ACT!

I will admit that I am guilty of improperly reflecting upon my weight. I know the only way the weight will come off is if I do something about it like exercise or making some key changes to my diet. Instead, I grab a bag of potato chips and a bowl of vanilla ice cream to dip the chips in (don't knock it until you try it). It's not complete until I have a tall glass of ice cold Coca-Cola to wash it all down, while I sit on the couch and watch TV. There's no doubt I acted, it was just the wrong action. The goal was to lose, not add to my weight. The reality is we know how we should act, but because we don't want to go through the trouble or pain and we don't want to put in the time or work, so we settle for something else.

> *The reality is we know how we should act, but because we don't want to go through the trouble or pain and there's no possible way we want to put the time or work in so we settle for something else.*

Esther could have acted in many different ways, she could have fled the palace and told all her people to go into exile. What good would that do? The decree was sealed.

We are told Abigail acted quickly, and she did so after reflecting quickly. She knew Nabal wasn't going to do anything about David and his men making their way to their home to finish them off. She knew he wasn't going to change his mind and say, "Honey, I was wrong. Prepare some food, David is coming with his men." Remember, this was a different age and time. She wasn't living in our generation where, if we women want to work, we work or if we want a career, we get a career. If we want kids, we have kids and if we don't, well then we don't. She didn't have her own money to spend on the food. She was living in a time when it was quite possible that the only reason this beautiful and intelligent woman married a man such as Nabal could have been because he purchased her. Everything she had was dependent on her husband and there wasn't much room for debate. She couldn't zip into a burger joint on the way to David; she had to take food that had been prepared for her household. When she realized danger was coming to her and her family, she reflected, which caused her to react...quickly!

So the baton was now passed to Abigail. She listened to what had happened and reacted by grabbing two hundred of this, one hundred of that and so on. Remember, it was for David and four hundred men.

Sometimes the answer to our problem is right under our nose, but often we're so busy focusing on the pain, or even worse, someone else's life that we miss out on being an 'Abigail' for our families. Remember, Abigail could have chosen to complain about the decision her husband had made and told him how dumb it was. She could have sat and let fear overcome her as she thought about how angry her surly husband would get for her acting without his permission. She could have sat worrying about how long it had taken to prepare the food that she was about to give away. She could have decided upon many different actions, however, she decided upon the simplest course of action: Feed the hungry men and do it quickly.

If you're a mother, maybe you can relate. Can you think of those moments where the baby wakes up in the middle of the night and you are so tired that you can't quite think so you start rocking the baby, singing to the baby, taking action in every way you can and nothing seems to help? Why? It is the wrong kind of action for a baby that just wants a dry diaper and a full belly. The sleepy mother hasn't taken the time to reflect, instead she just reacts. She wants the baby to go back to sleep so she can sleep. In her moment of action (jumping out of bed to retrieve the crying baby), if she takes even a brief moment to reflect (wake up just enough to think clearly), she will realize exactly what the baby wants and her goal will come to pass (sleep will be achieved).

Again, I must stress the importance of reflecting and acting. Sometimes they come one after the other, and sometimes they go hand in hand. They are both necessary tools for being a wise woman.

Maybe you are currently in a situation that seems out of your hands. Maybe you have taken the necessary time of reflection and the only thing time has given you is time to imagine how miserably you could fail. So you decide to do nothing. Fear has a way of halting our reaction time.

Not too long ago, my husband and I led a life group at our church based on his book, Excuses, Excuses, Which one is yours? The focus of the group, much like the book, was to realize that it doesn't take much effort to have an excuse to get out of something; in fact, it comes quite naturally. In order to move forward and react in life, we have to recognize those excuses and cut them off wa-ca-cha (those who know my husband will know what that means). We presented all the attendees with a homework assignment.

They were to write down their lame excuse for not serving to their full potential.

Our goal with this assignment was the following:
- Get them to reflect
- Cause them to act
- Be honest with themselves
- Give them permission to search within
- Be able to tell the difference between an excuse and a reason

Our hope was that this assignment would help them see what was really holding them back from serving to their full potential. Maybe it was fear to fail or maybe it was just laziness. We didn't ask them to read it out loud because we didn't want to put anyone on the spot to share if they were not ready to.

After the life group, one of the young women brought us her paper and said, "I want to read you and Peter my excuse because I want someone to help me be accountable so I don't use it." Here is what she read to us:

> What's my lame excuse for not serving to my full potential? Who am I? I want to write books, but I don't have the time to write them the way they need to be written. Then when I get past that, I look at other books and think, 'Why should I write?' There are thousands of amazing authors out there already. Who would want to read my work? Who am I? I want to do something for God. I want to allow God to flow through my words both speaking and writing and see Him touch people like I know He can. But then I think who am I? I'm just another person, a face in the crowd. I'm just another voice adding to the noise. There is nothing special about me. And that's the truth and that's my excuse and it keeps me stuck here. **BUT...**

> The real truth is that is what I hear in my head. What I hear in my heart is 'You are stronger and can bear much more than you realize, so don't be afraid when people unload. You are creative and can see things differently so don't be afraid to give input and change the

simple things. You've got a voice and things need to be said. And sometimes the weight of the words that flow through you seem heavy because you try to hold back the weight of them for others instead of setting aside how they will take them and receive them and instead simply letting them go.'

So I guess my super lame excuse is really this...I'm afraid to jump into the unknown, in faith, because I believe God is going to do something so crazy and so amazing and it really freaks me out. That's the truth, that's my excuse.

Our reaction to her letter: Wow! Mission accomplished! She was able to come to the realization that she has so much more to give and she was the only one in her way.

Often in our lives, in order to react, we will have to replace our fears with faith. Look at Queen Esther. Her first moment of reflection made it very clear that action was pointless, at least in her mind. We can see when she responds to Mordecai with fear, "The king has not called me for a while, and if I go before him I can die." But then after some more reflection, and a reality check from Mordecai, she decides to take the right kind of action. She decides to step out in faith.

Faith is the confidence that what we hope for will actually happen; it gives us assurance about things we cannot see. (Hebrews 11:1)

Esther looked at the situation through her eyes and said, "It's impossible, I'm going to fail," but when she stepped back and looked at the bigger picture, she realized it wasn't about her. With God, nothing is impossible! Notice when Esther realized the task at hand was bigger than her, she asks Mordecai to have everyone fast and pray before she proceeds. She is believing God would give her favor. I'm sure she was without fear. When she said "If I die, I die," she was totally putting her trust in God. Those words assured me that Esther wasn't some super powered wonder woman who could go through anything with a smile. She was a regular woman, just like you and I. She wanted to do what was right. She wanted to trust and believe God would handle it, but she also knew the results if God chose not to intervene on her behalf. And yet, she still chose to set her fears aside and react with faith.

When I think back to God speaking to me, "There are women who are hungry and you need to feed them. "There are women who are thirsty and you need to give them drink," I could have just laughed and said "You've got the wrong girl." Who was I to do anything for women? I was never the young girl who thought of myself as a princess. I was "one of the boys." My brothers would call me "that a boy," does that sound like a woman called to help women? I never wanted to play dress-up or with dolls. I grew up with six brothers and a sister. There were many times my mom had to force me to come inside to play dolls with my sister. All I wanted to do was be outside playing with my younger brothers, or even better, playing tackle football against the boys up the street. I remember a time when my mom called me inside to play with my sister, Marilyn. Reluctantly I went in, grabbed my Barbie by her feet, and hit her against the floor while crying, "I don't want to play with dolls." When Barbie's head fell off from the beating and rolled across the floor, I thought it was the funniest thing. My sister? Not so much.

Why would God call me to work with women? Why would He call Esther to save a nation? Why would He call Abigail to save her household? We were all 'just' women living life and minding our own business. If I would have given in to fear or failure, I wouldn't have positioned myself for God to do great things through me and through Complete Ministries, which was founded in 2004. Hundreds of women have been blessed, encouraged, empowered and healed because I chose to act and to obey God.

Maybe that's where you are right now. God has laid something important or special on your heart and you're thinking, "I'm just a woman" or "I'm just me." It might be something as simple as writing someone a note or as huge as moving across states. No matter the size or complexity of the task, maybe you're sitting here reading this thinking, "Well, there is this one thing but I'm just me. What can I do?" Esther went from thinking "What difference could I make" to "I can make a difference." What will your story be?

Wise women do not react upon who they are and in their own abilities but instead who they are in God and everything He has deposited in them for their journey. We all can, and probably will, have a million fears that will try to hold us back or make us think we cannot or should not move forward. But often those fears come from looking at ourselves through our eyes, rather than looking at ourselves through God's eyes.

I'm pretty sure there's a mirror in your purse. We look at it to make sure our lipstick is not outside the lines, our make-up isn't running, our hair is just right. Many of us will not leave the house until we look at ourselves in a long mirror so we can see ourselves from head to toe. And if we're completely honest, we walk by a mirror or a reflective glass and you know we are checking ourselves out! Why? To make sure everything looks good so that when others look at us, they see us well put together. We will look and depending on what we see, we act. Many times that means changing our outfit. This is what the word of God will do for us if we take the time to reflect and act on it daily so that we can live a life pleasing to Him. Looking at ourselves through God's eyes, seeing who we are through His word is so important in helping us act appropriately.

Leonardo da Vinci once said: "I love those who can smile in trouble, who can gather strength from distress, and grow brave by reflection. Tis the business of little minds to shrink, but they whose heart is firm, and whose conscience approves their conduct, will pursue their principles unto death."

I'm pretty confident that Da Vinci didn't write this with Abigail or Esther in mind, but he could have. 'Tis the business of little minds to shrink?' When we look at things through our own eyes and think, "What can I possible do?" will cause us to give up before we even try to react. That is why it is so important for us to replace our fears with faith. Yes, I said it again.

Esther had to face her fears. In doing so, she replaced her fear with faith. Abigail also had to face her fears and in doing so, she was able to come face-to-face with the man who wanted her and her family dead. In my case, I've had to replace my fears with faith and in doing so, I have been able to help so many women during the past 10 years.

Now it's your turn, say it out loud: I have to face my fears. I will replace my fears with faith. I will trust God and He will see me through.

If you didn't say it out loud, please do, as there is something powerful that happens when we declare and speak it into existence.

By doing this, we will gain courage to react to any news that comes our way. If God is able to do for you in a small situation, will you limit Him to not do for you and yours in the big situations?

A wise woman has the courage to act, and an even wiser woman takes the right action, no matter what the odds say.

Getting wisdom is the wisest thing you can do!
And whatever else you do, develop good judgment.
Proverbs 4:7

ACTION 3 | SACRIFICE

Abigail wasted no time. She quickly gathered 200 loaves of bread, two wineskins full of wine, five sheep that had been slaughtered, nearly a bushel of roasted grain, 100 clusters of raisins and 200 fig cakes. She packed them on donkeys and said to her servants, "Go on ahead. I will follow you shortly." But she didn't tell her husband, Nabal, what she was doing. (1 Samuel 25:18-19)

Exercising the courage to act is not always an easy task. Action requires us to do something. While there are many different actions that women can take, sometimes there are moments when God requires our actions to go one step further. These moments are known as sacrifices.

1 Chronicles 21:22-24 we find King David trying to purchase a threshing floor from Araunah. *²²David said to Araunah, "Let me buy this threshing floor from you at its full price. Then I will build an altar to the LORD there, so that he*

will stop the plague."[23] *"Take it, my lord the king, and use it as you wish," Araunah said to David. "I will give the oxen for the burnt offerings, and the threshing boards for wood to build a fire on the altar, and the wheat for the grain offering. I will give it all to you."* [24] *But King David replied to Araunah, "No, I insist on buying it for the full price. I will not take what is yours and give it to the* LORD. *I will not present burnt offerings that have cost me nothing!"* That's the kind of sacrifice I'm referring to, a sacrifice that will cost you something. Araunah wanted to give it to him but David knew it had to cost him something. Webster's dictionary defines sacrifice as the act of giving up something you want to keep, especially in order to get or do something else or to help someone. A sacrifice is something that cost you something. It's not like you having 10 pairs and shoes and you give a pair away. There's no sacrifice in that, you still have 9 pairs to choose from.

Abigail didn't just prepare a plate for David, she knew he wasn't coming alone so she prepared a large amount of food. Taking him a plate of food was all that seemed to be required. That in itself would have been a sacrifice because she would be going against her husband's wishes. But then there was that matter of those men with David, those 400 mighty men. Think of eight NFL football teams, with 53 active players on each team. Now I think you've got the picture. Think about those huge guys that play in the Super Bowl. Think about having to feed all of them, times four. Abigail's husband was wealthy so I'm sure it wouldn't have broken the bank to feed all those men. But again, remember, Abigail was not living in our time. She couldn't run to the grocery store and buy three or four shopping carts full of food. The food she was taking had been prepared for their sheep-shearing men. You guessed it, a bunch of people were going to be working hard to shear sheep and she is about to take a good chunk of their food and bring it to David and his men. That was a sacrifice!

There was an angry army marching toward her house to destroy it. It would have been great if she had her own personal army to protect her family and her workers, but unfortunately she didn't. She had to evaluate what she did have and sacrifice from that. She prepared that food in faith that it would allow her to get what she really needed, which was David to change his mind.

Have you ever told God, "I'll give more when I have more?" Maybe God is asking you to be more involved in a ministry and you respond, "I don't have the time because..." or maybe He's been telling you to forgive that person who hurt you and you respond, "I just can't because..." Is that not the same as saying, "I'll give more when I have more?" "I'll help out more when I don't feel as busy," "I'll forgive when I don't feel so hurt."

Abigail could have looked at her servant and said, "I don't have what I need for this situation so I guess we should all prepare to die." The same goes for Queen Esther, except she actually did respond to Mordecai with "What can I do?"

In Mark Chapter 12:41-44, we are told of a widow:

Jesus sat down near the collection box in the Temple and watched as the crowds dropped in their money. Many rich people put in large amounts. Then a poor widow came and dropped in two small coins. Jesus called his disciples to him and said, "I tell you the truth, this poor widow has given more than all the others who are making contributions. For they gave a tiny part of their surplus, but she, poor as she is, has given everything she had to live on."

A wise woman prepares a sacrifice with her whole heart. The story in Mark is often referenced when it comes to giving money. But if we look at the story word for word, Jesus speaks little about the money and volumes on the sacrifice, telling his disciples, *this poor widow has given more than all the others who are making contributions.* She just gave all that she had to live on? I would say that is a sacrifice. I see many people wanting to hang on to that last bit of money they had to survive, but not this widow.

This widow made a sacrifice that had no apparent return. I believe this widow made a sacrifice out of her love for God and her faith in him. If those two small coins were all she had to live on, maybe she thought, Here you go, God, you can do more with these coins than I can. I'll trust you.

If those two small coins were all she had to live on, maybe she thought, 'Here you go, God, you can do more with these coins than I can. I'll trust you.

Sounds a bit like Esther. Knowing she could die, she prepares herself as a sacrifice and decides to go before the king to plead for the lives of an entire nation. It also sounds a bit like Abigail who prepares a sacrifice of food in hopes to find favor with David and spare the lives of those in her household.

This is what I have come to learn; preparing a sacrifice is all about preparing your heart to give. You don't do things like that, just because! You sacrifice, because you trust God and you're obedient.

I went to a Women Thou Art Loosed Conference in Texas some years ago with some girlfriends. We were so excited to see what God had planned for us. T.D. Jakes was the scheduled speaker, but to our surprise a change in schedule was announced. Prophetess Juanita Bynum was going to preach. We were all super excited to hear her share God's word. She shared a powerful testimony that touched my heart and spirit. I knew in that moment that I had to give an offering, which would wind up being a sacrifice.

I had two checks with me, one to purchase the CD/DVD's so I could enjoy them again at a later time and the other for whatever might come up. Well, I realized that the 'whatever check' was for sowing a seed. As Prophetess Juanita Bynum continued sharing her story, my hands felt like they were burning. I wanted to release the check, I wanted to give my seed, but I still didn't know the amount I should give. About 20 minutes later she says "sow $1,000." I can honestly say, I didn't even think twice about the amount, I just knew as soon as she said the amount, I was going to sow it. I wrote that check out and practically ran it to the stage with excitement, knowing the Holy Spirit was speaking to me and I wanted to be quick to obey. After the service ended, my friends and I continued talking about how blessed we were and how impactful the word had been. That's when I came to the realization that I had just handed over a $1,000 check and hadn't even told my husband.

I quickly called him up and began sharing how powerful the word was that we had just heard. Then, with slight hesitation I told him, "I sowed a seed." He asked how much so I told him the amount and he then responded, "If that's what you felt you should give, then God will bless us for it." It was a relief to know that he agreed with me, especially since it was after I had already given it, but I wasn't too surprised by his response because he has always had a giver's heart. What did surprise me was God's response, because of my obedience.

Two months later, I was let go from my full-time job. We went from two incomes to a one–income household. This caught us off-guard and we quickly had to make changes to adapt to this new lifestyle.

Have you ever done something for someone and you remember you helped him or her out but they seem to have forgotten? Guess what, God never forgets!

When you prepare a sacrifice from your heart and give it to God out of love and obedience, chances are, you will forget about that sacrifice shortly after giving it. Why? Because a wise woman sacrifices out of love, not out of what she can get in return. Because of my experiences, I can promise you God will not forget about your love and obedience. He will remember you right when you need to be remembered.

Abigail didn't want to see her household perish so she prepared a sacrifice. Esther didn't want to see her people perish, so she prepared a sacrifice. In fact, both of them went against the normal traditions and stepped out to become sacrifices.

Be the 'Abigail' and 'Esther' of today. What storyline has God written for you? Are you ready to take the lead role? What are you waiting for? This is your season. Don't let it pass you by. Step out in faith, trust and obey God and give the sacrifice He is asking of you. If He called you, you can be sure He will see you through.

During our one-income season, it was as if God was saying remember that time you gave to me? Sit back and see how good I'm going to take care of you. My husband's car really needed new tires, something that was not in the budget. We were leading a small group of young married couples in our home and the guys from the group told him they wanted to detail his car. They brought the car back, not just nicely detailed, but with four new tires! Women would stop by and give us groceries and they always had my favorite drink, Coca-Cola. People would bless us with love offerings. Our children didn't get sick, things didn't break down. Time after time, we saw how God took good care of us during that season. He had taken our act of love and obedience and turned it into something more.

In the previous chapter, we talked about reacting in faith, not fear. Faith in God will not fail you. In the same way, preparing a sacrifice in faith will not leave you lacking. When you give to God, even though you may not intend to get anything in return, He will acknowledge your sacrifice when you least expect it.

God understands sacrifices. He sent his ONLY son to die for a group of sinners (well, it was a pretty large group — all of mankind). But still, it was his ONLY son, his BELOVED son. God could have simply said, 'Forget those people,' but He understood that those sinners (you and I) would forever be separated from His presence if a sacrifice was not made. He gave us Jesus and I'm so glad He did.

This is the example we must remember in our own giving. Wise women sacrifices with their whole heart. They give, knowing God will bless the sacrifice they have prepared, regardless of how big or small.

Teach us to realize the brevity of life,
so that we may grow in wisdom.
Psalms 90:12

ACTION 4 | HUMBLE YOURSELF AND SPEAK WITH WISDOM

As she was riding her donkey into a mountain ravine, she saw David and his men coming toward her. David had just been saying, "A lot of good it did to help this fellow. We protected his flocks in the wilderness, and nothing he owned was lost or stolen. But he has repaid me evil for good. May God strike me and kill me if even one man of his household is still alive tomorrow morning!" When Abigail saw David, she quickly got off her donkey and bowed low before him. She fell at his feet and said, "I accept all blame in this matter, my lord. Please listen to what I have to say. I know Nabal is a wicked and ill-tempered man; please don't pay any attention to him. He is a fool, just as his name suggests. But I never even saw the young men you sent." (1 Samuel 25:20-24)

A wise woman learns to humble herself and speak with wisdom. Notice I said learns. This doesn't come too natural for us. We either learn the easy way or the hard way.

There have been times when my husband has told me, "Honey, it's not what you say, it's how you say it." For example, the simple phrase "I told you so" has the potential to be good or bad. You can simply say "I told you so" in a tone that is nice, polite, sweet and encouraging. Then again, it could be said in a harsh tone. For example, "If you would have listened. I told you so," shaking your head and rolling your eyes in disgust.

He's right, but don't tell him I admitted it. Why is it that we can be so sweet, kind, patient and nice to everyone else but when it comes to our own, we are so quick to speak and too impatient to just stop and listen? As my dad would say when he would preach, "Just say ouch!" I hope someone can relate with me because it's true.

There were several studies done by Dr. Albert Mehrabian on the subject of nonverbal communication. In those studies, he found that 7% of any message is conveyed through words, 38% through certain vocal elements and 55% through non-verbal elements (facial expressions, gestures, posture, etc.). So perhaps there is some great wisdom when my husband says, "It's not the words we choose but how we choose to use them."

A wise woman will not only choose her words wisely, she will use the right tone of voice. This goes beyond our conversations. Let me explain. I was visiting a church and a lady was reading Ephesians 5:21-30 that says, *²¹ And further, submit to one another out of reverence for Christ, ²² for wives, this means submit to your husbands as to the Lord. ²³ For a husband is the head of his wife as Christ is the head of the church. He is the Savior of his body, the church. ²⁴ As the church submits to Christ, so you wives should submit to your husbands in everything ²⁵ For husbands, this means love your wives, just as Christ loved the church. He gave up his life for her ²⁶ to make her holy and clean, washed by the cleansing of God's word. ²⁷ He did this to present her to himself as a glorious church without a spot or wrinkle or any other blemish. Instead, she will be holy and without fault. ²⁸ In the same way, husbands ought to love their wives as they love their own bodies. For a man who loves his wife actually shows love for himself. ²⁹ No one hates his own body but feeds and cares for it, just as Christ cares for the church. ³⁰ And we are members of his body.*

> *A wise woman will not only choose her words wisely, she will use the right tone of voice.*

I'm happy to say that because of my relationship with my husband, I have no problem submitting to him so I wasn't bothered by the subject matter. However, I got bothered when she read it because of the tone in which she read it. It was so annoying to me that I just didn't want to listen to her, but I had no choice because I was taught to revere

God's Word. There was no going to the bathroom for me at that moment. I looked over at my mom and said, "Does she always sound like this?" My mom just looked at me with the 'girl, be quiet, they're reading the word' look. It was her tone that was bothering me because it was making me feel obligated and God's word wasn't obligating me.

Then there's how my mom prays! I love to hear my mom pray. She speaks to God in such a personable way and her tone is so soothing that if we're going to pray together, I can't pray next to her because I would just listen to her prayers.

In my life, I have prepared for moments by rehearsing what I should say on the way to meet someone. What kind of rehearsing could have been going through Abigail's head as she rode toward David? After all, she wasn't going to meet up with a friend or relative. She wasn't bringing cookies to the new neighbor. She was riding to meet with someone who was charging toward her home to kill everyone in it.

Life comes at us in many different directions, but remember all of these situations have an expiration date; they will come to an end. What can never expire is you speaking life to whatever it is you're facing. If speaking life is a new term for you, what I mean is staying positive and making sure that the words we speak are in favor of what we are believing God for and most importantly that they line up with His Word.

Have you been angry with someone because you played out in your mind what you expected he or she would say before they even said a word to you? Remember in chapter one when we talked about reflecting on the right things? What do you think could have happened if Abigail spent the entire donkey ride focusing on the fact that David was going to kill her family because he was hungry, and if when she reached him she went all LATINA on him! Mira que te pasa. Estás loco. ¿Tú no piensas? Porque no te dio de comer ahora vienes con toda intención de no solo matarlo a él pero a toda mi familia. Tu estas bien mal sabe! (That was in Spanish, in case you were wondering). Translation... what is wrong with you? Are you crazy? You don't think? Just because he didn't give you food you come all up in here with every intention of not just killing him but all of his family! Let's think about that for a moment! Yeah, I don't see that ending very well, do you?

Anyone can freak out on someone for doing something they don't like. What makes this story special is Abigail does the opposite. She humbles herself. Instead of approaching David with insults and threats, she approaches him with humility and kindness. We see Abigail not only speaking with wisdom, but acting with wisdom, as well.

She falls at his feet, she agrees with him that her husband is a fool, and then it's almost as if she turns into a Snickers commercial. She says, "David, I brought food. Eat, you're not yourself when you're hungry." Okay, maybe not so much on the Snickers commercial but through her wise actions and words, Abigail was able to open David's eyes and caused him to think (reflect) about what he was doing.

How? Abigail captured his attention so much so that he forgot he was hungry!

A wise woman can change the course for herself and her family when her focus is set correctly. Speaking with wisdom is often difficult when you are focusing on the problem rather than the solution. Instead of focusing on the impending doom, Abigail focused on getting David some food. Instead of focusing on the impending doom, Esther focused on presenting herself to the king. What is your impending doom? How are you reacting? You probably don't have four hundred mighty men charging to kill your family, or the weight of an entire nation's fate on your shoulders. However, in your own way you are also faced with impending doom just as these women were. It could be a bill due when the balance in your bank account says, "It ain't happening." A sick family member that's not expected to live long. A job loss when you're already barely surviving with the income you have. Maybe you have a child who is consuming all of your time because of their health or you spend all your time worrying about them because they are defiant, rebellious and disobedient. Never start believing God can't handle your situation. He is able! He can and He will. Let me say this in my preaching voice, "God is able to do all that He promised to do. Can I get an Amen?"

It is important in these times to make sure our focus remains on the solution rather than the problem. Whatever our focus is set on will most likely be the thing to grow. Think about it. Have you ever faced a situation and focused on the situation? Maybe you blamed God or someone else for the situation, or maybe you threw yourself a pity party. Where did it get you? How did it work out for you in the end?

Whatever our focus is set on will most likely be the thing to grow.

In order to speak with wisdom, we must first humble ourselves before God. Humbling ourselves before God will help to set our focus on the solution rather than the problem. When our focus is on God, we can begin to speak His word into our situation instead of our worries. We will be able to walk in His way instead of our own. Then we will see Him work in our favor.

It's not easy to humble ourselves. I know. There have been quite a few times when I got so upset at one of my children and instead of breathing, counting to 10 or reflecting on the power of my words, I would just lash out at them. At the time, it felt like the right thing to do. They got me upset and they should know better right? Wrong! After I would slam their room door and make it back to my room, the Holy Spirit would convict me. Remember Proverbs 14:1 "*A wise woman builds her home, but a foolish woman tears it down with her own hands."* I had no problem lashing out at them but somehow to go back in their room and apologize for how I spoke seemed like it was below me. However, I would go back in their room and do what I should have done in the first place, make it a learning moment with love and compassion. Use that situation as a learning moment. I didn't leave that room until I apologized and reminded them how much I loved them and how I only wanted them to succeed in life. There were those times that I knew I couldn't speak so I would write them a letter. This parenting thing isn't easy. Being a wife isn't easy, but it's all possible. I like to remind myself how much God trusts me to bless me with three handsome, respectful and loving boys. As long as they're in my care, I am responsible for their upbringing, and I want to do the best job I possibly can. For that, I need God's help.

We've seen how Abigail humbled herself and spoke with wisdom. Now, let's look at Esther. If you remember, we left off with Esther telling Mordecai to have all the Jews fast and pray for three days. Well, the time had come for her to approach King Xerxes. Esther walks into the throne room and to her relief, the king raises his scepter to approve of her visit. Esther walks toward the king and he asks, 'What do you want Queen Esther? What is your request? I will give it to you even if it is half the kingdom.'

Wait, what? She walked into this situation fearing for her life and she is now being offered half the kingdom? If Esther wasn't humble and selfless, this story could have taken a different route. The king had let his guard down. Maybe upon seeing her he had thought, "What could be so important to her that she would risk her life in coming before me?" or, maybe he was still captivated by her beauty? Whatever the reason, the king had offered to give her up to half the kingdom.

Let's glance at another story in Matthew 14.

When Herod Antipas, the ruler of Galilee, heard about Jesus, ²he said to his advisers, "This must be John the Baptist raised from the dead! That is why he can do such miracles.³ For Herod had arrested and imprisoned John as a favor to his wife Herodias (the former wife of Herod's brother Philip). ⁴ John had been telling Herod, "It is against God's law for you to marry her." ⁵ Herod wanted to kill John, but he was afraid of a riot, because all the people believed John was a prophet. ⁶ But at a birthday party for Herod, Herodias's daughter performed a dance that greatly pleased him, ⁷ so he promised with a vow to give her anything she wanted. ⁸ At her mother's urging, the girl said, "I want the head of John the Baptist on a tray!" ⁹ Then the king regretted what he had said; but because of the vow he had made in front of his guests, he issued the necessary orders. ¹⁰ So John was beheaded in the prison, ¹¹ and his head was brought on a tray and given to the girl, who took it to her mother. ¹² Later, John's disciples came for his body and buried it. Then they went and told Jesus what had happened.

Be careful what you promise. Because of King Herod's promise and the urging of her mother, she asks for John the

Baptist head on a platter. Herodia uses her daughter and manipulates the situation so she can get what she wants. What's worse is that the daughter willfully goes along with her mother's manipulative plan. This is proof that our children are watching us and will often follow in our footsteps, as well as take a few extra on their own. This mother and daughter used manipulation to achieve their selfish desires. Neither of these actions are present in a wise women's toolbox of actions.

It's amazing how women have this gift — let me rephrase that, the curse of manipulation. See, anyone can use words for their own selfish gain. A wise woman will use words for God's gain and glory. They speak words of life. Words to uplift, restore, and revive. Esther had the same beauty as Herodias' daughter and then some! How do you think that out of all the new queen candidates, King Xerxes' eyes were drawn to Esther?

Unlike Herodias, Esther approached the king with a selfless mindset. She had presented herself on behalf of others and not for her own benefit. Esther requested that King Xerxes and Haman attend a banquet she had prepared. Again with the food. Perhaps my mother was onto something when she said *"Fill a man's stomach before you start a conversation."* The king and Haman both arrived at the banquet, but it was obvious the king realized something was troubling Esther. He asks again, "What do you really want? What is your request?" Then once again, he offers her half the kingdom.

I like her response to the king, "This is my request and deepest wish. If I have found favor with the king, and if it pleases the king to grant my request, please come with Haman tomorrow to the banquet I will prepare for you." Esther is speaking with wisdom and I'm sure her tone is smooth and pleasant to the ear. She says, "Then I will explain what this is all about."

Esther could have told the king what she wanted at that moment, but perhaps she had a feeling that it wasn't the right time. She wasn't eager to get the situation over with, she wanted to handle it correctly and so she invites them back for another banquet.

King Xerxes left the banquet that evening with questions unanswered. Maybe that is why he had trouble sleeping that night. Since he couldn't sleep, he asked someone to begin reading to him from the book of his reign. How would you like people to document every detail of your life so you could read it over at a later time? While they were reading to him, they came upon the story of Mordecai saving the king's life after he uncovered a plot to assassinate the king. Coincidence? I think not!

Let me stop and say that Hollywood doesn't have anything on the Bible. They could never write a better screenplay than this story right here! It's got everything from tragedy, to romance, hope, pride, suspense, and action! You see Esther, Mordecai, King Xerxes, and Haman, all of them branching out into their own moments in the spotlight, and yet all four of them collide with each other. Esther is the unknown relative of Mordecai, Haman is the archenemy of Mordecai, and King Xerxes somehow got stuck in the middle of all the drama.

And if you don't think it's full of drama, let's go back to the banquet. Esther spoke to both men and when they went home that night, they take two entirely different paths. King Xerxes listens to a story of Mordecai saving his life and begins to wonder how he can best appreciate him for this gesture. Haman, on the other hand, sees Mordecai as ruining his life and plots how he can best annihilate him and his kind.

See, when Haman left the banquet, he was in high spirits thinking of everything the king had put him in charge of. He was delighted by all of it until he saw Mordecai sitting at the gate on his way home. This reminded Haman of the fact that Mordecai didn't treat him like the bigshot he thought he was. He went home and complained to his wife and friends and they agreed something should be done. They suggested he build a gallow to hang Mordecai, talk to the king about his plans, and happily to go the second banquet.

Seems to me like this is an excellent example of why having wise counsel is so very important. To which I say, "Thank you Jesus for blessing me with my mom." I remember when my dad felt his time was coming near to retire as lead pastor of our growing church in Milford, MA and there was a big possibility for my husband and I to lead it. I was a PK (pastor's kid) so I saw the good, the bad and the real ugly of some "Christian people." When I was old enough to pray for a husband, I would ask God that he, my future husband, be someone who would love God, love me and not have the calling to be a pastor. An evangelist would be okay, but not a pastor. Well I thought we had a deal, but God had other plans. A few months before this became "real," my mom knew something was bothering me and she just prayed for me and of course her prayer was a-ma-zing. After her prayer she looked at me and said, "Soly (that's my nickname), make sure you keep God first, your family second and the church third." Her wise counsel helped, and continues to help me. When I saw that my kids were feeling resentful because I was spending too much time at church or with members from the church, her words would resonate loud and clear and I would make the necessary changes. There were many times when she would say to me, "Drop off the boys and go spend time with your husband." I always took her up on it. Her wise counsel helped me make sure I was a wife and mom first and reminded me of how important they were to me. I can testify today that my boys love me, love their dad, and more importantly, they love God!

For some reason, Haman thought the idea he discussed with his wife and friends was a good one. The next morning, before he could tell the king of his plans to hang Mordecai, the king asked him how he could best honor someone he wanted to recognize. Haman, thinking that person would be himself, gives the king a grand idea to honor somebody.

Unfortunately for Haman that somebody the king was referring to was Mordecai. So instead of talking with the king about his plot to hang Mordecai, Haman wound up leading Mordecai around the city on one of the king's finest horses, while he was dressed in the king's robes, and Haman shouted, "Here is a man the king delights to honor." Talk about humiliation.

I'm sure Haman was happy to at least have that second banquet to attend. That is until Esther tells the king that she only asks for her life and the lives of her people to be spared. When the king asks who would do such a thing, she points to Haman.

The king had just honored Mordecai, a Jewish man, for his loyalty. He had just found out that his queen, whom he loved dearly, was also of Jewish descent. To top it all off, he had just been told that Haman, who he thought to be someone of good counsel, had signed a proclamation with the king's seal of approval to annihilate all Jews.

Talk about a double, maybe even triple, slap in the face! Would the king have felt as betrayed if Esther had told him what was bothering her at the first banquet? Who knows? All I know is that Esther humbled herself and spoke with wisdom on more than one account. This wisdom gained her favor in the king's eyes. Favor that her people needed in order to escape their inevitable doom.

As wise women, we need to be very careful with the thoughts we allow in our minds. Our thoughts are often the deciding factors on how we will react. Our thoughts can often blind us and take us down the wrong road. Look at David, so blinded by hunger and disrespect that he sets out to kill a household. Or Haman, so blinded by pride and how he thought he should be treated that he was willing to annihilate a race of people to prove he was someone of importance. Let's not forget Herodias' daughter, so blinded by the love of her mother that she doesn't question whether her deadly request is right or wrong.

Then there are those who have their minds set on the right thoughts, like Abigail who disregards the charging men and does what she knows is right. Or Esther, who stays focused on the lives of others instead of dwelling on the importance of her own.

Its clear God knows that we will have days when our thought will get out of hand. So He reminds us in Romans 12:2, *"Don't copy the behavior and customs of this world."* What does that mean? Well, what does the world do? When doom is bearing down, some may run and hide, because they value their own lives. Some might pout and say how unfair such a matter is when tough situations arise. Others might charge into the situation ready to throw a fit if necessary to prove they are somebody. *...but let God transform you into a new person by changing the way you think.* How can changing the way we think transform us? How can it humble us and help us to speak with wisdom?

Just like Abigail and Esther, if we choose to focus on what needs to be done, rather than what's about to be done, we will find ourselves becoming the solution, rather than looking for a solution. That is what I believe is being spoken when the Bible says, *"Then you will learn to know God's will for you."* What do we have to do to know God's will for us? We have to stop copying the world and instead let God transform us.

It's not an easy thing to stop copying the world. Copying the world comes naturally. Allowing God to transform us comes only through humility. The kind of humility found when we throw our hands up and say, "Jesus, take the wheel." James 4:10 talks about having that kind of humility in our time of need, as well, *"Let yourself be brought low before the Lord. Then He will lift you up and help you."* Another translation says *"humble yourself."* Rather than coming across a situation and trying to figure out how best we can handle it, maybe it's best for us to humble ourselves and realize God will handle it a lot better.

In Genesis, God says He is going to make man in His image. Then later in the Bible, it says that God is love (1 John 4:8). If we have been made in the image of God and God is love, then maybe we should know a little bit about love. I mean, how can we ever "be transformed" if we don't know what to transform into? So what is love? Well, let's go over to 1 Corinthians 13:4-7 and find out:

Love is patient and kind. Love is not jealous or boastful or proud or rude. It does not demand its own way. It is not irritable, and it keeps no record of being wronged. It does not rejoice about injustice, but rejoices whenever the truth wins out. Love never gives up, never loses faith, is always hopeful, and endures through every circumstance.

The attributes listed in these verses describe love. Therefore they also describe God, and the image we should strive to follow. After reading through the verses, I can see where they could easily be used to describe Abigail and Esther. Both of these women displayed love in their time of reflection. Both of these women thought of others instead of demanding their own way. Both of these women decided to endure their circumstances and to never lose faith. So I would conclude that both of these women were operating with love. Both of these women were operating in God's will. When we choose to operate in God's will, we will see God's favor.

Not only does Abigail humble herself and speak with wisdom, she prophesied:

> *"Now, my lord, as surely as the Lord lives and you yourself live, since the Lord has kept you from murdering and taking vengeance into your own hands, let all your enemies and those who try to harm you be as cursed as Nabal is. (1 Samuel 25:26-27)*

She is aware of whom David is, and that there is a special calling (anointing) on him. It was no secret that David had killed many men, and even a giant in his time. She is also aware that the actions he is about to carry out will be seen much differently from his 'victories' and she reminds him of this by prophesying over him. She didn't call him a fool for his crazy actions. Instead, she spoke with wisdom. She spoke to him about how great God was for keeping David from his current plans. The funny thing is, she is speaking to him not knowing if he would change his mind, but BELIEVING he would. If that is not speaking with wisdom, I'm not sure what is. How different would our lives be if every time someone opposed us, we prophesied over them about who God had called them to be rather than calling them out for who they were being in that moment? I want to be like Abigail when I grow up!

I think Abigail knew David, being the macho man he was, wasn't going to soften up with a few kind words or a simple plea. She tells David not to worry about Nabal because he is a fool, she makes him think about his own foolish actions by speaking about him not doing them, and then she redirects him to the food that has been brought.

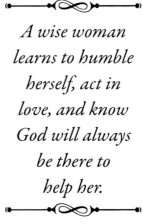

A wise woman learns to humble herself, act in love, and know God will always be there to help her.

A wise woman learns to humble herself, act in love, and know God will always be there to help her. She also allows God to fill her mouth with wisdom. She understands the truth found in Luke 21:15, *"for I will give you the right words and such wisdom that none of your opponents will be able to reply or refute you!"* She speaks God's word over herself, her family, her surroundings, her enemies and her future.

Live wisely among those who are not believers,
and make the most of every opportunity. Let your
conversation be gracious and attractive so that you will
have the right response for everyone.
Colossians 4:5-6

ACTION 5 | FORGIVENESS

Please forgive me if I have offended you in any way. (1 Samuel 25:28)

I am quite aware there are more actions than the seven referenced in this book. That being said, I do believe that if we start to apply these seven, our lives and the lives of everyone around us will change and it will only get easier to make wiser decisions.

Maybe your thought is, these are all good but I don't have the time to apply these seven, so I'll just choose one. If that's you, well allow me to suggest forgiveness. Webster's Dictionary defines forgiveness:

Forgive: to stop feeling anger toward (someone who has done something wrong): to stop blaming (someone). To stop feeling anger about (something): to forgive someone for (something wrong), to stop requiring payment of (money that is owed).

Why would I suggest this action? My main reason would be Matthew 6:14-15 *"If you forgive those who sin against you, your heavenly Father will forgive you. But if you refuse to forgive others, your Father will not forgive your sins."*

That first half of the verse is music to my ears. The second half of that verse doesn't sound so great, but we can't take certain parts of the verse and disregard the other.

I like Abigail's approach to asking for forgiveness. I'm not saying this is the only way to do it, but it seemed to work great in her situation. The first thing she says after she falls to her knees is, *"I beg you, forgive the sin of your woman servant."* Was she at fault for what was happening? No, not at all! But rather than adding fire to the flame, she decided to be the solution.

In the previous chapter, we talked about the importance of our words. As I write this, I chuckle because my middle son, Jonathyn, gets bothered when I tell him, "Don't say always" or "Never say never." Those two words can quickly change the course of a conversation. Why take this time with Jonathyn? I am trying to teach him something I'm still learning to apply in my life with the hopes of him learning it at a younger age and being equipped to make better decisions. I tell him, "Jonathyn when you're having a conversation with your girlfriend or wife, try not to use the words 'you always' or 'you never,' and instead use the words 'I feel as if you' or 'when you say that, I feel.' Speaking of things or circumstances in this manner removes *all* of the blame from the other person and puts *some* of the blame on you. When we say things like "you always," I find that it is often because we have kept a tally somewhere we shouldn't have. Think about it, when you make statements like, "You always say that," are you saying it because you want to help the person change the way they are talking or are you saying it because you're tired of hearing the way they are talking?

See, sometimes we think forgiveness is a one-and-done deal when forgiveness is more of a lifestyle. Picture this, there is a woman who has lived her entire life on pennies. Then one day she strikes it rich. She's not living off the dollar menu anymore. In fact, she isn't even visiting restaurants with a dollar menu. Then one day she wakes up and forgets she's rich. She walks into the nearest restaurant and goes right back to using that dollar menu.

How in the world could she just forget she was rich? How could she just wake up and go right back to doing things the way she use to? It's easy, we do it all the time!

That is what James is saying in Chapter 1: *"For if you listen to the word and don't obey, it is like glancing at your face in a mirror. You see yourself, walk away, and forget what you look like. But if you look carefully into the perfect law that sets you free, and if you do what it says and don't forget what you heard, then God will bless you for doing it." (James 1:23-25)*

See, using words like "you always" and "you never" show we are keeping track of things. And like I said, it's usually not the good things we are tracking. So what does this mean?

It means we started out eating off of the dollar menu. God offered us his great riches (forgiveness), which was something we needed, but didn't fully understand. Instead of letting those riches (forgiveness) change who we are, we continue to run back to that silly dollar menu (old ways) because it's what we are used to.

This is why I say forgiveness has to be a lifestyle. We cannot simply use it as a one-and-done.

Have you ever told a toddler or young child to "say you're sorry?" Most of them have no idea what they're saying, but we feel better if they say it right? I know God has looked down on me from his throne and has told me "say you're sorry" and although I didn't want to, I said it so that He would leave me alone. (As if I had fooled Him to think I meant it). Just like there have been times when He has said, "Say you're sorry" and I have responded "No! Why do they get to hurt me, and I have to say I'm sorry? They hurt me too, let them come and say they're sorry."

If you thought I was pretty close to perfect, then think again, I'm still on this path of learning perfection right alongside you. I've succeeded at times but I also have failed. The truth is a wise woman will learn how to embrace this lifestyle of forgiveness and walk it out daily rather than use it one day and throw it out the next.

As I'm still on the path of learning, let's use other examples of people, who once they understood this lifestyle of forgiveness, gave it freely. People who heard "God has forgiven you now forgive others in the same manner" and walked it out without even giving it a second thought. One of those people was Stephen from the New Testament. People are stoning him and he says "Forgive them." Maybe Stephen got to see Jesus hanging on the cross asking the Father to forgive the people who were murdering him. Maybe that is why he so quickly decided to do the same to those who were trying to kill him. I don't know. But I do know there are people who still embrace this lifestyle today. Not because they got to see it firsthand, but because they've read God's word and embraced forgiveness as a lifestyle.

I can remember hearing the story of Yiye Avila, an Evangelist widely known in Hispanic culture. One of his daughters was murdered by her husband and he forgave the man. Why would he do that? Because he had embraced a lifestyle of forgiveness.

I have had the privilege of witnessing this kind of lifestyle in my own family. My dad was the pastor of a church and I remember when a member got upset with him and knocked him to the ground right outside the church. My brothers and I saw this all happen so we ran to where he was. He looked at us, asked us to help him up, and take him to the altar. When he got there, my dad fell to his knees and asked God to forgive the man. This was definitely one of those lessons where actions spoke louder than words.

I'm aware of Matthew 6:14-15. I don't know it by heart, and I cannot quote it word for word, but I fully understand the meaning of what it says. I rejoice in the fact that our heavenly Father has forgiven me of all of my nonsense (iniquities) and regrets (sins), but when it comes time for me to pay it forward, it's not that easy. Throughout my life, I have come face to face with moments where I had to decide if I was going to stand on God's word and offer forgiveness, or if I was going to stand on my own stubborn pride and say "No way!" I had taught kids in Sunday school what forgiveness was, and I had even counseled married couples on the importance of forgiving and forgetting. I remember telling them, "I know it's easier said than done," but I didn't know how hard it actually was to forgive until I began facing these moments in my own life.

Have you ever had those moments? Moments where people you thought you could trust betrayed you? Moments where people who once had your back now pointed their fingers and shot accusations? Or maybe even moments where you just felt wronged and you just didn't even want to see those people anymore?

Isn't it just like the enemy to throw a curveball at you when you're prepared for a fastball? That curveball just comes out of nowhere and suddenly not hitting it is all you can think about. I'm not going to sugar coat it. When moments like this have hit my life it has caught me off guard, to say the least. There were times when I couldn't eat or sleep. I was caught so off guard by the wrongs that I couldn't find a right. Have you been there?

Isn't it funny how we know what the Bible says but somehow that knowledge goes straight out the door the moment we are in a position to apply scripture? The Bible says to forgive those who wrong us, but is that really the first thing that pops into your mind at the time?

If that's you, let me applaud and tell you to continue doing what you're doing because it's not the first thing that pops into my mind. Remember, I'm learning and growing. In my growth, I have learned to humbly admit my wrongs. It isn't as easy as I thought it would be because I have been so hurt that I didn't even want to think about what the Word said. Instead, I just wanted to scroll through Facebook and hit unfriend, unfriend, unfriend...and oh this one person, remove completely. Reflecting back at those moments, I see how unfair it

> *Those hurtful moments had blanketed me in a sunburn of bitterness and I was throwing myself a pity party.*

was to assume their posts, looks, and whispers were about me. Those hurtful moments had blanketed me in a sunburn of bitterness and I was throwing myself a pity party. You know what that's like when you're so tender that every...little... thing...just rubs you the wrong way? Even when people try to make things right, you take it wrong.

Well if you can relate, then you my friend, have had a moment of un-forgiveness. Even when someone made a comment to make me feel better, I found myself disgusted at the fact that they had even tried. They couldn't possibly understand my situation. You've been there, too? Oh, Lord, give us strength to get through this chapter.

What Abigail and Esther were facing was rough. Physical death was approaching their door. I believe un-forgiveness can bring something worse; spiritual death. See, a spiritual death often happens slowly. It happens with one pout here and one eye roll there until you find yourself in a miserably bitter pit that only God has a rope long enough to reach down and bring you up. I'm telling you this is not good because the longer you allow yourself to continue in this state, the worse it can get.

Imagine finding a small curious bump on your arm one morning and instead of going to an expert to have it looked at or simply getting rid of it you decide it's no big deal. A little more time goes by and you've gotten used to the bump, in fact, it's quite normal for you to have around now. You soon notice your arm begins to hurt around the bump, but again you shrug it off and ignore it. Eventually, you find yourself two years down the road sitting in a doctor's office and your entire body feels like a giant bruise and after many questions from the doctor, you conclude that this whole situation started with a small bump. What makes matters worse is that the doctor informs you that had you come in and had the bump removed when you found it, you would not be facing the pain you are in now.

So why in the world would we ever hold on to hurt and bitterness? Why not release it with forgiveness? Well that is because it's easier to hold on to the hurt and bitterness! It's crazy but we have no issue holding a grudge because it is a part of our selfish, sinful nature. Our selfish nature wants to be pitied, it wants to stay angry, and it hopes to see the people who hurt us suffer. It's sad because what we don't realize is that each of these actions are stepping stones taking us further from God and closer to spiritual death. Each of these wrongful, negative actions we seem to enjoy because we think they make *us* feel better, are creating a lifestyle of criticism rather than a lifestyle that mirrors God.

Something that I have come to realize through my moments of un-forgiveness was that Satan enjoys, he delights, in playing on our emotions. Let's stop him from feeling so delightful. Being a Christian is about surrendering control to God. Satan knows this so he begins using other people in our lives to distract us. We cannot control what other people say and do to us. It's important you understand that. Don't lose anymore sleep over them, just pray for them. What we do have control over are our actions and sad but true, often times were unwilling to forgive.

I don't know about you but I don't like myself in those moments. Why wasn't forgiveness as easy as I had made it sound to those Sunday school kids and married couples? Because forgiveness was not my lifestyle, just words on a page. Until these difficult, hurtful moments arose in my life, I never had to work my forgiveness muscles. I was like a hiker who had fallen and now found myself hanging from the side of a cliff, regretting that I hadn't spent more time doing pull-ups.

When we are faced with situations that are out of our control, we find out real fast where our faith is. We also discover our internal scoreboard. See, we may think our spirit has the lead, but I can guarantee the moment a situation is thrown at you and it's out of your control, that's the moment you will see reality for what it is.

I've come to realize the moments where my flesh added points to the scoreboard and I was totally unaware they were racking up. Those were the moments when my prayers sounded like, "God, help me to forgive them. I know it's the right thing to do but I just want them to hurt like I hurt. I want them to lose like I've lost. God, it's just not fair! Boohoo, please feel sorry for me."

What I couldn't see was God sitting in his comfy chair, looking down saying, "Well, if you read my word then you would know how I feel about you. I don't feel sorry for you, I call you blessed." *"God blesses you when people mock you and persecute you and lie about you and say all sorts of evil things against you because you are my followers. Be happy about it! Be very glad! For a great reward awaits you in heaven. And remember, the ancient prophets were persecuted in the same way." (Matthew 5:11-12)*

That can be a hard thing to swallow. Here's what these verses do not mean: they do not mean that God doesn't care, they do not mean that God delights in your misfortune, and they do not mean you are left alone in your painful state of sorrow. So what does that scripture mean? It means this: being a Christian is not some ticket to a life of luxury. Just like for Esther living in the palace didn't exempt her from the impending doom Haman had decreed. The moment you become a Christian, you have put yourself on the most wanted list of Hell. You've been added to Satan's hit list, you've become the irritating ingrown nail on Satan's big toe. However in all things count it all joy! God will never leave us or forsake us, and with Him on our side, we win!

Before you start questioning your choice to follow God, let me remind you of someone — Jesus. He lived his life out so we would have an example on how this is done. We are told that in this life we would have affliction, but to have peace because He has overcome the world. (Read John 16:33 and Romans 12:12). Not on our own strength, by any means, but through the Holy Spirit, which is here to be our helper on Earth.

A wise woman must recognize that her strength does not come from her own abilities and skills but from God. When she recognizes that, other things will set themselves straight in her life. Holding a grudge won't be an option because God doesn't hold grudges. Not forgiving those who wronged us won't be an option, because God forgives, period, exclamation point!

I can't write this and tell you I've gotten it right every time. Just ask my husband and children. What I can tell you is that every time I leaned on God, He made it right! Every time I found myself not having the strength to forgive, God provided me with the strength. Every time I thought the hurt was too much to bear, I gave it to God and found myself without the burden.

Abigail asks for forgiveness when she has done nothing wrong. Abigail didn't know if David would even let her speak, but she obviously wanted him to know that she knew he had been wronged. As Christians, sometimes we must realize it is not just those who have wronged us who need to be offered forgiveness. Sometimes it is also those who have been wronged. Sometimes they just need to see compassion in their fury. Abigail stepped up to stand for what she believed in. When she did, she didn't accuse David of being a mad man, she related to him. She was helping him reflect so he could act wisely.

She asked David to forgive her for the wrong done against him. Stop for a few minutes and allow the Holy Spirit to bring to your memory those people you have yet to forgive. Don't rush through this either, allow the Holy Spirit to speak to your heart so you can forgive and be free. We all have people that have hurt us, but we hide those memories deep in our subconscious because we don't want to deal with the pain. Today is the day you release all your past pain, hurt, bitterness, anger, and anything else that holds you back.

Surrender everything at the feet of the cross! Today you are free in Jesus name. Be wise! Humble yourself and ask for forgiveness even if you feel it wasn't your fault. Save your marriage, save your relationship with your child or sibling or friend. Life is too short here on this side of heaven to coincide with un-forgiveness and hurt. Don't move on to the next chapter until you have resolved this. If you need help, open your Bible and let God heal you through His word. Free yourself and watch you grow!

Allow me to close this chapter with another scripture found in Matthew 18:22, Jesus answered, '*I tell you, not seven times but 77 times.*" This is not a one-and-done deal. We have freely been given forgiveness by our Father, now let's pay it forward. A wise woman has been forgiven by God so a wise woman offers forgiveness. She doesn't wear it as the trending fashion of the day; she embraces it as a lifestyle! Forgiveness is a choice and that choice is yours. Choose wisely.

But the wisdom from above is first of all pure.
It is also peace loving, gentle at all times, and willing to
yield to others. It is full of mercy and the fruit of good
deeds. It shows no favoritism and is always sincere.

James 3:17

ACTION 6 | STAND IN THE GAP

"Even when you are chased by those who seek to kill you, your life is safe in the care of the Lord your God, secure in his treasure pouch! But the lives of your enemies will disappear like stones shot from a sling! When the Lord has done all he promised and has made you leader of Israel, don't let this be a blemish on your record. Then your conscience won't have to bear the staggering burden of needless bloodshed and vengeance. And when the Lord has done these great things for you, please remember me, your servant!" (1 Samuel 25:29-31)

Have you ever seen a movie and it has that moment when the bad guys are charging toward the good guys and that one person courageously says, "Go! I'll hold them back?" That's what I think of when I hear "stand in the gap."

As moviegoers, we hear that person saying, "Go! I'll hold them off!" but shortly after we might forget how important the action of that person was. Because if the person didn't hold them off, they wouldn't have gotten away.

Standing in the gap simply means interceding. It means that just like in the movies when a person holds the door so the others can get away, we do the same but instead we cover them in prayer. We stand firm during the trial or temptation and we're not giving up on them because we trust God to make a way. Now the character who says, "Go! I'll hold them off!" often dies in the movie, but in real life, when we intercede, that's not the case. We stand in the gap believing the trial will die, the temptation will cease, our children will be the man or woman God called them to be, and above all we believe the enemy will be defeated in Jesus name.

I liked the explanation I found on www.myredeemer-lives.com where it says, *"Think of a brick wall, in particular, the mortar in the joints between the bricks. That mortar 'goes between,' or 'intercedes'" between the bricks to bind them together and strengthen them. Without the mortar 'going between' the bricks, the wall would collapse. If you want to break down that wall, the easiest way is to start where there are gaps in the mortar. You start chopping and chipping at those sections, and soon the entire wall will lack the support it needs and will give way."*

As wise women, we have to be ready to stand in the gap for our marriages, our families and for others. How exactly

do we do that? By choosing to live a life of prayer and inter-
cession. www.myredeemerlives.com continued, "*The Enemy
does not target the areas where we're strong; that would be spiritual suicide for them. He targets our weaknesses, our vulnera-
bilities, our besetting sins [our friends & family members may
not know about them, but the spiritual forces in the heavenly
places do!]. They look for old recently healed or not-yet-healed
emotional wounds, or habits about which we feel some shame or
guilt [like smoking, gluttony, too much TV, too much internet
or social networking, etc.], or those matters we've confessed to
others as being weaknesses or problems in our lives. So, when
we intercede for one another, our chief purpose is to fill in those
gaps in one another's spiritual armor and hold up that person so
the enemy can't gain an advantage over them. Likewise, when
we fail to intercede for one another, we're virtually giving the
key to that person's spiritual house to his/her enemies for them
to wreak havoc, to steal that person's peace or joy or health or
even their financial security. Just as we wouldn't build a brick
wall and intentionally leave gaping holes in the cement joints, I
would go so far as to say it's malicious for us to not 'go between' /
'stand in the gap' for our brothers, sisters, and our religious and
political leaders. Jesus said, 'By this all shall know that you are
my disciples, if you have love toward one another.' [John 13:35]
How can we say we love one another and not pray for each
other? It's impossible! It's a contradiction and a lie!*"

We know Esther and her people prayed and fasted for
three days. I believe as Abigail rode her donkey to face David,

she prayed. They were both facing death and yet they chose to stand in the gap.

Maybe you are in a situation where it seems like you're pinned between two negatives. If you go to the left, you'll be wrong and if you go to the right, you'll be wrong. So what can you possibly do? You can go down on your knees. There is always a way out.

Abigail wasn't only standing in the gap for her family, but also for David's future. He was anointed king over all of Israel and if he went along with his plan, he would have innocent blood on his hands. David wasn't at war with Nabal, he was angry and he was reacting out of his anger. Did Nabal deserve to die for denying him food? Absolutely not! David lost his temper and Nabal and his family were going to pay for his temper tantrum.

Abigail begins to speak to him in such a way that David listens. She has captured his attention. I love how she says, *"Since the Lord has kept you from murdering and taking vengeance into your own hands."* David's plan had not yet changed, but since the power of life and death is in our tongue, she begins to speak as if it were the case. She reminds him, Nabal is a cursed man. She brings David's attention to the fact that he was hungry, so she points to the food she had sent with her servant.

Abigail apologizes, even though it wasn't her fault. She speaks of his destiny and even stretches the truth, saying he hasn't done anything wrong in his entire life. However, we can think of a few "wrongs" he committed. Although she didn't know what had happened between him and King Saul in 1 Samuel Chapter 24, where he had the chance to kill but instead he cuts a corner of King Saul's robe and walks away. Abigail reminds him he is a man with a good heart.

I can imagine David's shoulders release from the tightness and his angry face soften as her words spoke over him. You go, Abigail!

They have a clear understanding of what could happen to them if they continued to go in the direction they chose; yet they don't deviate from it. Abigail gets on her donkey and makes her way to David. Esther says I'm going for it, I will present myself before the king and if I die, then I die. That's courage. We need that kind of courage.

I'm reminded of another group of wise women in the Bible. Although they were not facing death, they were going to lose a lot if they didn't stand in the gap. In Numbers 26, a census is taken in order to determine who gets what in the Promised Land. If you remember the story of the twelve spies sent to scout Canaan a.k.a the Promised Land (Numbers 13) and ten of the spies reported back saying, "We seemed like grasshoppers in our own eyes, and we looked the same to them" while Joshua and Caleb had stood by God's promise that the land was theirs. That bad report left the Israelites wandering around in the desert for forty years. Then here we come to this census. The census is to determine how the land will be divided among the second generation of Israelites, a.k.a the wilderness survivors.

In Numbers 27, we learn of a man named Zelophehad who had died in the wilderness but wasn't with the company of men who had gathered together against God. According to the census, which only counted male descendants, his family wouldn't be receiving a piece of the land. That news didn't set well with his five daughters, so they did something that wasn't too common for women of their day...they stood in the gap. They went before Moses, the priest, and the leaders, and they made their appeal. "Why should the name of our father disappear from his clan just because he had no sons? Give us property along with the rest of our relatives." (Numbers 27:4)

Their father hadn't done anything wrong, he just died and now his family was going to be forgotten and their inheritance lost. All because he didn't have any sons? That just didn't seem fair. So they made their appeal and Moses took their appeal to God. God replied: (v.6-11) *"The claim of the daughters of Zelophehad is legitimate. You must give them a grant of land along with their father's relatives. Assign them the property that would have been given to their father. And give the following instructions to the people of Israel: If a man dies and has no son, then give his inheritance to his daughters. And if he has no daughter either, transfer his inheritance to his brothers. If he has no brothers, give his inheritance to his father's brothers. But if his father has no brothers, give his inheritance to the nearest relative in his clan. This is a legal requirement for the people of Israel, just as the Lord commanded Moses."*

Instead of accepting the chain of events that were given to them, these women decided to stand in the gap in the hopes of making a change.

They didn't just decide on a whim to stand before Moses, Eleazer, and everyone else. They thought this through (they reflected), because the outcome could be that they would be ridiculed and mocked for years to come. They spoke with wisdom, stating who their father was and although he wasn't perfect, his inheritance should not be forgotten just because he had no sons. These weren't your average women. These women were wise and they were willing to stand in the gap for what they believed was right! And in doing so, they not only changed the future of their own inheritance, but the future of other families' inheritances as well.

We are not told how the sisters felt when the response was, "*You too will receive your inheritance.*" I'm sure it was a day of excitement, joy and a day that changed history. If they hadn't stood up and spoken up, they would have lost their inheritance.

Standing in the gap can happen in many different ways. For some, it may be waking up at 5 a.m. to go before the Lord and pray. Maybe it's showing "tough love" to a child. Maybe your faith is being tested and challenged? Maybe you see your husband so overprotective with his phone and it causes you to think he's hiding something from you? What do you do? The question should be; what have you done? You probably threw Action 1 (reflecting) right out of the window and went straight to Action 2 (acting), and now your situation is worse.

I'm here to tell you it's still not too late! Don't give up just yet. Learn to be like a boxer preparing for a big match. He takes the time to prepare and he makes all kinds of sacrifices because he has a prize to win. Don't think you don't have the time either. See things are different. Now you make the time to go before the Lord and fight for what is yours! Don't sit back! Today is the day you choose to stand in the gap. Regardless of the situation, you will stand firmly on the rock!

Abigail stood in the gap because the lives of her family members were at stake. Esther stood in the gap because the lives of many Jews were at stake. The daughters of Zelophehad stood in the gap because they were facing a loss that could lead to poverty. Can you think of any moments where you had to stand in the gap? Standing in the gap simply means you are going to take a stand for what is right. As parents, we tell our children to make good choices and be good examples to those around them. I'm sure our Heavenly Father is saying the same thing to us, "Don't be foolish, be a wise woman! Be willing to stand for what is right."

What would you do if God were to appear in one of your early morning prayers, those early prayers when you and God are the only ones awake, and He was to ask you, "What do you want?" Ask, and I will give it to you!" Would you be as spiritual as Solomon was when he was asked this question in 1 Kings Chapter 3? Come on; be honest with your response, after all, most likely you're alone as you read this. Out of all the things he could have asked for, and believe me there were a lot of other options, he chose wisdom. What I find interesting is that Solomon recognized he was in uncharted waters. This was a path unlike any he had ever experienced. He was doing what his father wanted him to do. He was building a temple for Jehovah. Not only was he building this temple, he was King over a nation that was chosen by God. Solomon finds himself as a child who doesn't know his way around so he asks for wisdom. Wisdom that would help him stand in the gap for others.

Solomon tells God, "*Give me an understanding heart so that I can govern your people well and know the difference between right and wrong. For who by himself is able to govern this great people of yours?*"

I've heard my husband, Peter, say time and time again, "Wisdom is knowing your limitations." Solomon knew his limitations. That's why he asked for wisdom. He decided to ask for something that would make him a valued asset to the throne. God was pleased with his request and so he tells him in 1 King 3:10-12 "*The Lord was pleased that Solomon had asked for wisdom. So God replied, 'Because you have asked for wisdom in governing my people with justice and have not asked for a long life or wealth or the death of your enemies—I will give you what you asked for! I will give you a wise and understanding heart such as no one else has had or ever will have.*"

That's pretty cool isn't it? God wasn't finished yet, he continues, "*And I will also give you what you did not ask for—riches and fame! No other king in all the world will be compared to you for the rest of your life!*" *(1 King 3:14)*

It's your story. You're not able to change the events that have already transpired, but you can surely change the outcome of future events. Be wise. Make the time to pray and intercede. Stand in the gap and watch God be faithful in return. We are called to be a wall around our family, let's be a strong wall.

Oh, how great are God's riches and wisdom and knowledge! How impossible it is for us to understand his decisions and his ways!

Romans 11:33

ACTION 7 |
REJOICE ALWAYS

"David replied to Abigail, 'Praise the Lord, the God of Israel, who has sent you to meet me today! Thank God for your good sense! Bless you for keeping me from murder and from carrying out vengeance with my own hands. For I swear by the Lord, the God of Israel, who has kept me from hurting you, that if you had not hurried out to meet me, not one of Nabal's men would still be alive tomorrow morning.' Then David accepted her present and told her, 'Return home in peace. I have heard what you said. We will not kill your husband." (1 Samuel 25:32-35)

Up to this point, I have mentioned a lot of actions that can help make us be wise like the Proverbs 14:1 woman. All, if not most of the previous actions might seem hard, but here's one that shouldn't be hard at all. A wise woman will rejoice. Not only in the good times, but always. This action is probably the most overlooked and it requires very little. In fact, this action requires such little sacrifice that I'm sure we just overlook it because of its simplicity.

Read this slowly so it really sets in: wise women make the time to rejoice. It could be a hallelujah and-a-hand-raise rejoicing moment or it can be a throw-a-party and-shout-because-God-got-you-through rejoicing moment

David received his food and says, "*Go home in peace. I have heard your words and grant your request.*" Now that's a throw-a-party-and-rejoice-because-God-has-brought-you-through-something moment.

Abigail returns home and Nabal is having his own kind of party. The Bible tells us that Nabal was in high spirits and very drunk, so she chose not to say anything until daybreak. Let me just add that, like Abigail, we, too, need to know when to speak and when no to speak. It's more difficult to be silent than to speak. At times, there's more wisdom in being silent.

The following morning as Abigail tells him what she did, his heart failed him and he became like stone. If that wasn't bad enough, 10 days later the Lord struck Nabal and he died. I know what you're thinking, "I thought this chapter was about rejoicing." Stay with me.

What was Abigail thinking about all of this? Unfortunately, she is not around to ask, but I don't believe it was a throw-a-party moment. If she wanted Nabal dead, she could have just fled and left Nabal to face David and his wrath. Instead, she faced David and saved her household.

I have had Philippians 4:4 in my heart for quite some time and I felt as if God was trying to show me something. The verse says, *"Rejoice in the Lord always. I will say it again: Rejoice!"* Simple right? Well no, not so simple. Many times we remember the rejoice part, so when good things happen, we rejoice. Well, good things don't always happen. I'm a pro at rejoicing when things are great, but I have failed to rejoice when things were not so great. The reason is because I didn't follow a very important part of the verse. It says, "Rejoice in the Lord always." The secret is to rejoice in the Lord, not just rejoice.

I mentioned early in the book that I'm from a family of eight siblings and we are all very close. Life as we knew it was great until May of 2008 came along. I was driving my trailblazer with my youngest son, Malachi, when my phone rang. I was happy when it was dad, but immediately I heard something different in his voice and my stomach sank. He asked me where I was headed, and I told him I was on my way home. He told me to go straight to my brother Steven's house. My thoughts were everywhere, my heart was racing and I just kept asking "Dad, what's wrong?" He of course didn't want to tell me as I was driving, but I wasn't letting him off the hook. I hear his voice break and I could hear him crying when he says, "Its Benji" I'm like, OK what happened to Ben, was he in an accident, what happened. My dad couldn't bring himself to say the words but I kept insisting and now I'm crying and begging him to tell me because I didn't want to drive and wonder. He finally gives in and says Benji's dead.

I heard him but I didn't hear him. I was like what? He said, "Soly, Benji passed away." I was in total disbelief. There was no way the youngest of our family had passed. I was asking a hundred questions. There was just no possible way. This just isn't true. This can't be true. I pulled over, and cried, yelled and totally freaked out. I kept punching the armrest until the buttons for the window broke. Suddenly, I hear a young voice call out, "Mommy." I forgot my Malachi, who was 5 years old at the time, was in the car with me. When I turned to look at him, he had tears rolling down his sweet face. Why wouldn't he, his mom totally lost it. He had no idea of what I just heard, he just saw me freak out. I practically jumped in the back seat and held him. I couldn't bring myself to tell my young son that his uncle passed away. I got back in the driver's seat and I headed to my brother, Steve's, house. When I arrived, my brothers were outside. I got out of my car, looked at them hoping they would tell me it was all a lie, but it wasn't. I realized that moment was the beginning of our lives being upside down and inside out. Life as we knew it would never, and I mean never, be the same. How could this possibly be a time to rejoice?

The days and weeks that followed were a blur. We were going through the motions. We all had to fly to Florida because he was living in Poinciana with his wife and two children. All sorts of arrangements had to be made. It was awful. I couldn't believe that a few days before Mother's Day, we would lay my brother Benjamin's body to rest. How do you rejoice? How can you rejoice?

Looking back now, I know God was with us because how can you go through something like that without God. In the midst of all the hurt and pain, there was also peace. We found moments of joy and laughter as we thought of Ben's life and how grateful we all were that God would give him to us for the years He did. In my pain, I began to realize my healing was in rejoicing in the Lord. It wasn't that I was to rejoice in the loss of my brother, but to rejoice in the Lord and all the good we received because He gave us Ben. For the amazing childhood we had, the unforgettable memories I will forever hold dear to my heart. For the many times we were able to share the gospel of Jesus Christ through music for more than 20 years and bless hundreds, if not thousands, of people. Rejoice in the fact that I can see him through his beautiful children, Simone and Silas. Rejoicing always is not an easy thing to do, but it's possible.

So when was Abigail's time to rejoice? Now she finds herself planning a funeral. Maybe Abigail's thoughts were, "What was the point of all this? I just took a big risk and for what? My husband is dead and now I'm a widow. Who will care for me?" Then again, I would like to think Abigail bailed out on the pity party and believed her God would still be with her despite her sudden turn of events. The thing about life is that if you're still living, it's still happening. She had already spoken life into the situation, now she had to wait for her harvest.

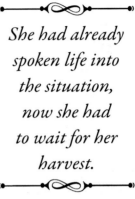

She had already spoken life into the situation, now she had to wait for her harvest.

In verse 31, Abigail leaves David with the following words "*Remember your servant.*" How could he forget the words of such a wise woman? Those words must have resonated in David, and when he heard Nabal had died, he said, *"Thanks be to the Lord, Who has punished Nabal for putting me to shame. He has kept His servant from sin. And the Lord has turned the sin of Nabal upon himself." Then David sent word to Abigail, asking her to be his wife.*

Start the music and let's celebrate! It was worth reflecting, acting, making the sacrifice, speaking with wisdom and humbling herself. It was worth asking for forgiveness and standing in the gap.

> *When David heard that Nabal was dead, he said, 'Praise the Lord, who has avenged the insult I received from Nabal and has kept me from doing it myself. Nabal has received the punishment for his sin.' Then David sent messengers to Abigail to ask her to become his wife. When the messengers arrived at Carmel, they*

told Abigail, 'David has sent us to take you back
to marry him.' She bowed low to the ground and
responded, 'I, your servant, would be happy to
marry David. I would even be willing to become
a slave, washing the feet of his servants!' Quickly
getting ready, she took along five of her servant
girls as attendants, mounted her donkey, and
went with David's messengers. And so she
became his wife. (1 Samuel 25:39-43)

Even David had a time of rejoicing because of Abigail's
wise counsel. He didn't shed innocent blood and God han-
dled the situation for him. Abigail went from being married
to a surly fool to marrying the future King of Israel. Now
that's a throw-a-party-and-rejoice moment for sure.

Esther's situation had a moment of rejoicing, as well, but
it didn't come as easy as it did for Abigail. You would think
that when King Xerxes had Haman killed, the bad guy would
be gone and the problem solved, right? Wrong! The decree
Haman had written was signed with the King's seal, which
meant it couldn't be erased and forgotten.

Then King Xerxes said to Queen Esther and
Mordecai the Jew, 'I have given Esther the
property of Haman, and he has been impaled
on a pole because he tried to destroy the Jews.
Now go ahead and send a message to the Jews

in the king's name, telling them whatever you want, and seal it with the king's signet ring. But remember that whatever has already been written in the king's name and sealed with his signet ring can never be revoked.' (Esther 8:7-8)

This part of Esther's story isn't spoken as much as her famous words, *'if I perish, I perish" (Esther 4:16)*. However, this is my favorite part of her story. Prior to this, their destiny was death, but now they were given an opportunity to fight and change their destiny. If you haven't read all of the Book of Esther, please make sure you do. You will see how the Jews were glad to have the authority and opportunity to fight.

The King's decree gave the Jews in every city authority to unite to defend their lives. They were allowed to kill, slaughter, and annihilate anyone of any nationality or province who might attack them or their children and wives, and to take the property of their enemies. (Esther 8:11)

For the Jews it was a time of joy and happiness and honor. In every part of the nation and in every city where the king's law had come, there was happiness and joy for the Jews, a special supper and a good day. And many people who

had come there from other countries became
Jews because they were afraid of the Jews.
(Vs 16-17)

I want to encourage and remind you that you have been given the authority to fight. So fight! What you have is worth fighting for. Don't surrender and never give up. A wise woman knows who her enemy is. If you don't know let me remind you of Ephesians 6:12 that says, *For we are not fighting against flesh-and-blood enemies but against evil rulers and authorities of the unseen world, against mighty powers in the dark world, and against evil spirits in the heavenly places.* The enemy wants us to think it's our husband, our children or maybe someone in the workplace because he wants us to give up. I encourage you to never give up. Grab a piece of paper and a pen and write Romans 8:37 down that says, *No, despite all these things, overwhelming victory is ours through Christ, who loved us.* Your marriage is worth fighting for, just stop fighting your husband. Your children are worth fighting for, just love on them. Overwhelming victory is ours, yes that's for you and me and it only comes through Christ who loves us dearly.

I'm very grateful and I rejoice when I think of the ten years we hosted Complete Woman Conferences in Milford, Massachusetts. I will continue what I started ten years ago and that is to encourage women to rejoice in 'their' today, regardless of what they're going through. When we're young, we can't wait to get older. We can't wait to graduate from high school. Then we graduate and while some think college, others think, "I need to get married, so when will that happen?" You get married and then it's when will we have children? I'm sure you know what I mean. We're too busy waiting and working for the next thing and we truly miss out on some happy moments.

The Word is clear when it says, *"This is the day that the Lord has made. We will rejoice and be glad in it." Psalm 118:24* Write that verse on your mirror so when you wake up and start your day, you are reminded that today is a gift from God, so rejoice! Enjoy it with those around you. Make peace with those who hurt you. Tomorrow is never promised. Let's be wise in planning for our tomorrow but rejoicing in our today.

This is a simple chapter because this is a simple action, but like I said, it is so simple that it can easily be overlooked. To rejoice means to be thankful. To rejoice means to stop and breath it all in. Maybe you're blessed to live in a house with a porch and a swing, so relax, sit down and swing away while enjoying God's beautiful landscape. Everything you have gone through has made you who you are today. If you don't like it, start embracing some of these actions and change your outcome. If you're happy, then continue what you're doing.

Rejoice in the small things. Rejoice in the big things. Rejoice before the storm, during the storm, and after the storm! God is good (all the time) so find it a joy to fight for what is yours. Find it a joy to live every day to its fullest and live every day as if it were your last. Make time to hug and love on your children, regardless of their age. Schedule date nights with your husband. Make those you love a priority and rejoice in your today.

So be careful how you live. Don't live like fools, but like those who are wise. Make the most of every opportunity in these evil days.

Ephesians 5:15-16

WHAT WILL YOUR STORY BE?

This book is not a checklist. It's not something where you take your pencil and start to check off your list and move on. These actions and many more are to be reviewed often. They are to help us walk this journey of faith and to help us grow. Will you make mistakes? It is likely, but you will reflect and act wisely. You will be obedient in your sacrifice. You will learn when to speak and when not to speak. You will forgive freely and not be afraid to stand in the gap for you, your marriage, your family, your career and especially your calling. You will learn to rejoice in the Lord always.

At the beginning of the book, I asked a question: "What are the actions that make a woman wise?" I said that in order to outline these actions, we would need a story. Because often times it is not one single moment that makes a woman wise or foolish, but rather a series of events that lead up to that moment, and what she then decides to do with that moment. We looked at the series of events that were laid out for Abigail and Esther and then we looked at what they did with their moments. Abigail's moment saved a household and gained a new husband. Esther's moment saved a nation.

What will your moment be?

God has given you your assignment, your moments, your story. Moments that have and will continue to shape your life. Moments that will write your story. This is why wisdom is so important in our lives. Think of your life as having many crossroads, a string of crazy highways. Wisdom will lead you in the right path but foolishness will take you down another. The truth is, your wisdom or foolishness won't only affect you, but everyone around you.

Don't let others write your story for you. It's your story! You're going to have to live through the heartache, the pain, the joy and victories. Since you have to live it, choose wisely.

Looking back at my life, I can now see some of those crossroads. One came when Peter and I were in our fifth year of marriage.

He worked two hours away from home, so he would leave Tuesday and get home Friday. To help save time and gas, he would stay with his aunt because she lived closer to where he worked. Meanwhile, I was at home caring for two little boys feeling as if I was carrying the whole world (my household and children) on my shoulders. I felt as if I was getting the bad end of the deal and these feelings caused conflict in my marriage. One night before he came home, I had thrown his clothes in a big garbage bag so when he came back home he could pick the bag up, turn right around and go live with his aunt. Well, my siblings got a hold of my plan and had an intervention. They were like Mordecai, helping me see the bigger picture, and thankfully, I realized they were right. Peter and I worked it out and thankfully we have been married (sometimes happily and sometimes not so happily) for more than 20 years. Yes that was a throw-a-party' moment for sure. From that crossroad, I can confirm, firsthand, that a wise woman takes time to reflect and she executes the right actions.

Another crossroad came at one of our Complete Woman Conferences. I remember one of the ladies came to me very excited because she was blessed at the event. She was just eager to share her excitement and wanted to let me know she would be back the following year. That year was a trying year for me personally, and in that moment I was so focused on what was happening in my personal life that I wasn't looking at the bigger picture, and so my response to her was quick and short. "I don't think there will be a next year." She didn't have to say a word because her face spoke volumes. I shrugged it off and walked away. On my way to the elevator, I kept seeing her reaction in my mind and I began to question if my actions were right.

I got to my room and I told my friend Melanie what happened. She quickly rebuked me. Then she did to me what I should have done to that women, she spoke life into me. She reminded me of the power of my words and once they're said, they're out. It was like taking a tube of toothpaste and squeezing it all out, there was no way I could get it back in the tube. The same is with our words, once we speak them, there is no way of taking them back. I realized that was a time to speak life to my situation but instead I spoke death. I was more focused on me than what God was doing in and through me to bless many lives that weekend.

The next morning during our prayer and praise time, I publicly asked for forgiveness. And to make a long story short, the woman I sucker punched with my words (that's how it felt to me), became vice president of Complete Ministries about two years after this incident and has been working side-by-side with me ever since, reaching women with the message that only Christ completes us.

I know there's a toolbox in your house somewhere, even if it's a kitchen drawer. The truth is you can't use a screwdriver to do what a hammer does. Every tool has its specific purpose. This book is like a toolbox filled with many actions. Don't disregard one or throw one away, they're all necessary in this journey. These are not one-and-done kind of actions. Just as I said about forgiveness, all of these actions are meant to become part of our lives and help shape who we are. When *you* allow these

When you allow these actions to shape you, they will begin to shape your story and mold it for God's glory.

actions to shape *you,* they will begin to shape your story and mold it for God's glory.

The stories of Abigail and Esther are just small moments taken from their lives. They lived before the stories that were recorded and they continued to live afterward. The same goes for you. You lived before this moment (good, bad, or seemingly impossible), and you will continue to live after this moment. You choose if you will be wise or foolish.

#CHOOSEWISDOM

ACKNOWLEDGMENTS

First and foremost, to our Lord and Savior, Jesus Christ! Thank you for blessing me with gifts and abilities and I pray they always glorify you.

To my husband, Peter and our three amazing boys: Peter Jacob, Jonathyn Andrew and Malachi Nick Lopez – you all complete me.

My siblings: Jessie, Orlando, Marilyn, Steven, Eliezer, Herson and Benjamin, (there will always be eight of us). I'm so glad I was born into this family! Wouldn't trade it for the world. To all of my in-laws, nephews and nieces. I love you all very much.

Amazing friends that have been with me through many ups and downs, (you know who you are). You put the best in the best of friends. Your friendship is priceless and I'm a better, happier and wiser person because of you.

Complete Ministries Team, past and present. Thank you for saying *yes* to volunteering in this amazing ministry, and for sharing this journey with me. I thank God for you and I pray the Lord rewards you a hundred fold for all your time, gifts you have invested and/or still continue to invest in Complete Ministries.

Thanks to Pastor Johana, Rev. J, Felisha, Leslie, Monica, Venus, LaShawnda, Maria, Patti and my sister Marilyn for your time, help and support during this project.

Special thanks to Nicole Donoho and Lee Nessel. I am so grateful God placed you both in my path for a season such as this. Forever grateful.

I want to thank Pastor Ken & Cher Hitte and all of my Discover Life Church family. Thank you for accepting me and my family with open, loving arms. Let's continue to Make Disciples: New Ones, Better Ones.

If you need wisdom, ask our generous God, and he will give it to you. He will not rebuke you for asking.

James 1:5

#CHOOSEWISDOM

Here are two stories to remind you of the importance of being a wise woman. You choose, just like these 10 bridesmaids did. They knew where they were going and whom they were going to meet, however, some prepared for the journey and some didn't. You are important to God! Whether you are single, married, divorced, separated or widowed. YOU are important to God, so be wise in your daily living so that when He comes for you, you will be ready.

Parable of the Ten Bridesmaids | Matthew 25:1-13

[1] "Then the Kingdom of Heaven will be like ten bridesmaids who took their lamps and went to meet the bridegroom. [2] Five of them were foolish, and five were wise. [3] The five who were foolish didn't take enough olive oil for their lamps, [4] but the other five were wise enough to take along extra oil. [5] When the bridegroom was delayed, they all became drowsy and fell asleep. [6] "At midnight they were roused by

the shout, 'Look, the bridegroom is coming! Come out and meet him!' [7] "All the bridesmaids got up and prepared their lamps. [8] Then the five foolish ones asked the others, 'Please give us some of your oil because our lamps are going out.' [9] "But the others replied, 'We don't have enough for all of us. Go to a shop and buy some for yourselves.' [10] "But while they were gone to buy oil, the bridegroom came. Then those who were ready went in with him to the marriage feast, and the door was locked. [11] Later, when the other five bridesmaids returned, they stood outside, calling, 'Lord! Lord! Open the door for us!' [12] "But he called back, 'Believe me, I don't know you!' [13] "So you, too, must keep watch! For you do not know the day or hour of my return.

#CHOOSEWISDOM

If God were to ask you, 'What do you want?' How would you answer?

Solomon was asked that very question and instead of asking for riches, wisdom and fame, he asked for wisdom. In asking for wisdom, he got all of the above and then some.

Solomon Asks for Wisdom | 2 Chronicles 1:1-12

[1] Solomon son of David took firm control of his kingdom, for the Lord his God was with him and made him very powerful. [2] Solomon called together all the leaders of Israel—the generals and captains of the army, the judges, and all the political and clan leaders. [3] Then he led the entire assembly to the place of worship in Gibeon, for God's Tabernacle was located there. (This was the Tabernacle that Moses, the Lord's servant, had made in the wilderness.) [4] David had already moved the Ark of God from Kiriath-jearim to the tent he had prepared for it in Jerusalem. [5] But the bronze

altar made by Bezalel son of Uri and grandson of Hur was there at Gibeon in front of the Tabernacle of the Lord. So Solomon and the people gathered in front of it to consult the Lord. [6] There in front of the Tabernacle, Solomon went up to the bronze altar in the Lord's presence and sacrificed 1,000 burnt offerings on it. [7] That night God appeared to Solomon and said, "What do you want? Ask, and I will give it to you!" [8] Solomon replied to God, "You showed great and faithful love to David, my father, and now you have made me king in his place. [9] O Lord God, please continue to keep your promise to David my father, for you have made me king over a people as numerous as the dust of the earth! [10] Give me the wisdom and knowledge to lead them properly, for who could possibly govern this great people of yours?" [11] God said to Solomon, "Because your greatest desire is to help your people, and you did not ask for wealth, riches, fame, or even the death of your enemies or a long life, but rather you asked for wisdom and knowledge to properly govern my people— [12] I will certainly give you the wisdom and knowledge you requested. But I will also give you wealth, riches, and fame such as no other king has had before you or will ever have in the future!"

Complete Ministries is a Christian, bilingual, organization that travels from city to city empowering, equipping and encouraging the Body of Christ. We are financially supported by contributions from friends and partners of the ministry.

Our goal is to share the Gospel of Jesus Christ
and help spread one simple message:
"Only Christ Completes Us."

It is ONLY through Him we are able to live Well,
Blessed and Complete.

Our Mission Is Simple...Love people where they are!

Jesus replied, 'you must love the Lord your God with all your heart, all your soul, and all your mind.' This is the first and greatest commandment. A second is equally important: 'Love your neighbor as yourself.' – Matthew 22:37-37

For the Complete Woman Story please visit
www.completeministries.org

ABOUT THE AUTHOR

Sorines was born in Rochester, NY on the 9th of December. Sorines is one of eight children born to Puerto Rican parents Jesus and Digna Gonzalez.

Sorines and her siblings shared the Gospel of Jesus Christ through song for over twenty years in the U.S. and Puerto Rico as The Gonzalez Brothers.

In 1994 she married Peter Lopez and has been blessed with three children: Peter Jacob aka PJ, Jonathyn Andrew and Malachi Nick.

In 2004, Sorines founded Complete Ministries, a Christian, bilingual, organization that travels from city to city empowering, equipping and encouraging the Body of Christ.

In 2009 Sorines was blessed to be one of the key worship leaders for Boston Night of Worship (BNOW) a worship movement where thousands of people from Boston, New England, and across the world gather in desperation to pursue the one true and living God, Jesus Christ.

Sorines is a wife, mother, singer/songwriter, conference speaker, and author. She is full of energy and passion when it comes to sharing the gospel of Jesus and see lives empowered and transformed. She delights in seeing women, as well as men, find their 'completeness' in Jesus.

NOTES

How much better to get wisdom than gold,
and good judgement than silver!
Proverbs 16:16

NOTES

Wise words bring approval, but fools are destroyed by their own words.

Ecclesiastes 10:12

NOTES

Pride leads to conflict; those who take advice are wise.

Proverbs 13:10